# FOALE AND TUFFIN

## The Sixties. A Decade in Fashion.
Iain R. Webb

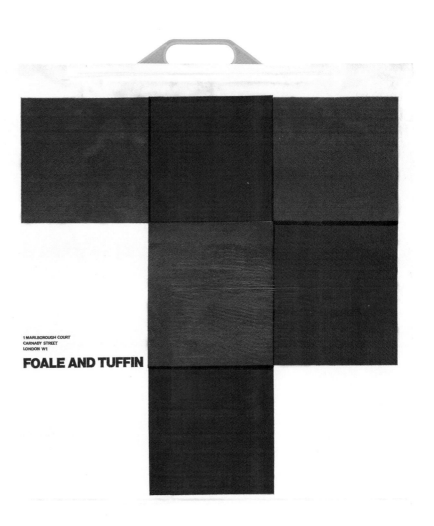

1 MARLBOROUGH COURT
CARNABY STREET
LONDON W1

**FOALE AND TUFFIN**

ISBN 978-1-85149-606-8

British Library Cataloguing-in-Publication Data. A catalogue record for this book is available from the British Library.

Publication designed and typeset by Northbank, Bath.

Printed in China.

Published in England by ACC Editions, a division of Antique Collectors' Club Ltd, Woodbridge, Suffolk.

**Marion and Sally would like to dedicate this book to their friend Marit Allen.**

Foale and Tuffin labels.

**Overleaf:** Publicity stunt featuring Sally (left) and Marion (second from left), 1963.

MARION FOALE AND SALLY TUFFIN MADE IN ENGLAND MARION FOALE AND SALLY TUFFIN MADE IN ENGLAND MA

ON FOALE LY TUFFIN MADE IN ENGLAND MARION FOALE AND SALLY TUFFIN MADE IN ENGLAND MARION AND SALLY

ALE FIN MADE IN ENGLAND MARION FOALE AND SALLY TUFFIN MADE IN ENGLAND MARION FOALE AND SALLY TUFFIN

# Contents

Foale and Tuffin Ltd stencil
for boutique shop window.

# TUFFIN

$\leftarrow$ 2" | 2¾" | 3" | 3½" | 4"  5 SIZES 2 prints ea

# LTD

H size $\rightarrow$

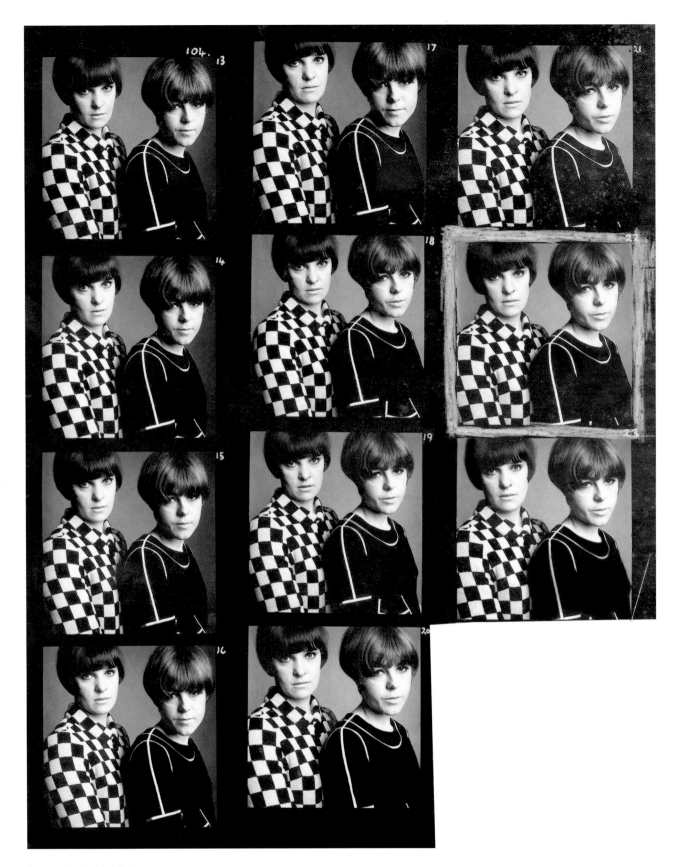

Contact sheet for Mod photo
session featuring Marion (left) and
Sally, 1964, *David Montgomery*.

# TAKE TWO

## COCKY
## FEISTY
## BOLSHY
## GIRLS

**Foreword**
Iain R. Webb

**Take two girls. Marion Foale and Sally Tuffin.** Two cocky, feisty, bolshy (as they like to describe themselves), 'kicky' (as the American press pictured them), arty, clever-clogs young women who at the beginning of the 1960s just happened to collide with fashion at the split second that they were needed. 'They make clothes that go with the times,' raved one fashion pundit. And it was true. The narrative of the Foale and Tuffin story perfectly traces the decade from its groovy, optimistic beginnings, when the two embryonic fashion designers blithely set up shop in 1961, to its demise, as sixties sanguinity melted away into a hangover of seventies cynicism, masked as it was by the distraction of fancy-dress escapism; the pair hung up their label in 1972.

Foale and Tuffin, the women and the label they formed, were *The Liver Birds* of fashion; although they might dislike the title there are pertinent parallels. Indeed, fashion writer Shirley Lowe once referred to them in the *Daily Mirror* as 'the designing birds'. 'Liver Birds' Dawn and Beryl (played respectively by Pauline Collins and Polly James) were groundbreaking both in the real world and on screen. Carla Lane's situation comedy was the first TV venture to centre around two female characters that embodied the brand new, liberated 'dolly birds'. Dawn and Beryl had the wherewithal to rent themselves somewhere to live (albeit a flat share situation – much of the comedy was the collision of their two backgrounds, middle and working class) and the attitude (one might again best describe as bolshy) to survive in what was still, regardless of the godsend of tights and the pill, very much a male dominated world.

Integral to the story was the intensely devoted relationship of the flatmates, just as it has been with Marion and Sally. 'Sally does most of the talking,' noted one journalist during an interview. '"But we always take decisions together," says Sally.'

The 1960s was a decade that began in black and white, a rollover from the 1950s. But the times they were a-changing. In 1960 John F Kennedy was elected as president of the United States, while the following year Yuri Gagarin orbited the earth in Vostok 1. It was a world that no longer had boundaries and it promised new universes to explore. Just like the Russian cosmonaut, Foale and Tuffin were rocketed into the spotlight of the media, which was itself replenished by the unshakeable self-confidence of youth. In June 1963 journalist Merry Archard wrote in a series of articles dedicated to the duo in the *Sunday Citizen* newspaper: 'In January last year just an old sewing machine and a few bolts of fabric stood between these two 25-year-olds and the dole queue. … Now they are big names in the fashion world.' In an aside the journalist noted that neither looked more than seventeen, 'both smoking king-size filter-tip cigarettes and giggling'.

Whether from working or middle class backgrounds, Marion and Sally were, like many others at the time, escaping the narrow vision of their environment and the straitjackets of their upbringing. For them the art school experience was not just about learning how to paint or draw or sew; it was more importantly an opportunity to embark on a new way of life. It provided a new world of possibilities and the chance to be with like-minded people, being witness to, and presented with, all manner of new stimuli. In January 1957 artist Richard Hamilton spelt out the new criteria for pop art that could have been the blueprint for the aspiring fashion duo: 'Pop art is: Popular (designed for a mass audience), Transient (short term solution), Expendable (easily forgotten), Low cost, Mass produced, Young (aimed at youth), Witty, Sexy, Gimmicky, Glamorous, Big business.' These were groundbreaking times, and the two young women designers embodied this Brave New World aesthetic right down to their shiny patent Moya Bowler shoes.

Marion and Sally were trailblazers. *Time* magazine described them as two of London's 'top happeners'. Having won the battle (and the places) to attend art school, first Walthamstow Art School in North East London (where several key long-term friendships were formed) and later the prestigious Royal College of Art (RCA) in Kensington, they relished the opportunities this provided, both artistic and extra-curricular. Stimulated by their new surroundings they blossomed and flourished, feeding on a diet of exacting training and the exciting imagery being proffered by their artistic contemporaries, who included Peter Blake, Derek Boshier and David Hockney. They were also fortunate to be encouraged by far-sighted teachers like Joanna Brogden, Bernard Nevill and Janey Ironside, who took over from Madge Garland

at the RCA in 1956, and rightly noted in her biography *Janey* that the duo were at the forefront of a new mood: '… when I first took over the school it was taken for granted that a student leaving would try to get a job in a manufacturing firm, this changed after Sally Tuffin and Marion Foale set up on their own, with a lot of courage, two hundred pounds loaned to them by Mrs Joy Bentall, and finally with success.'

For the friends, starting their own business was the only option, as they regarded the alternative 'stick-in-the-cloth job as assistant-assistant-assistant designer in a wholesale dress firm' as just too awful to contemplate. So, in 1961 Marion Foale and Sally Tuffin became officially Foale and Tuffin Ltd, working out of a West London bedsit.

For the most part Foale and Tuffin embodied the changing panorama in society. America may have invented teenagers but it was the British who dressed them. And so, petticoated ballerina skirts gave way to Capri pants and pencil skirts, and in time, to the minuscule little dresses that edged ever further above the knee in a break for freedom.

A new breed of British 'dolly bird' designers and working class lads – the likes of Mary Quant, Foale and Tuffin, Gerald McCann, Kiki Byrne, Alice Pollock, David Sassoon, Jean Muir at Jane and Jane, John Bates and Caroline Charles – were the antithesis of the 'posh blokes', and became the new arbiters of style. One such was Terence Conran, himself making his name in the world of interiors. Conran opened his Habitat emporium on the Fulham Road in 1964 and soon any self-respecting living room about town was filled with blond wood Scandinavian furniture, utilitarian pasta jars and orange Le Creuset cookware.

The backdrop of society was changing, quite literally. In 1965 in the *Observer* colour supplement (one of the 'new media'), Georgina Howell catalogued the shifting landscape, celebrating the emerging modernist architecture that was casting a new urban shadow by juxtaposing it with contemporary designer clothes. 'Our fashion editor has been finding new clothes to keep pace with the new architecture.' Previewing the latest fashions the feature noted that there were 'surprising new vistas and settings' springing up all over Britain: the escalators at the Elephant and Castle covered shopping centre; the Birmingham Bull Ring; St Paul's precinct ('the square is like a piece of New York dropped down beside St Paul's') and the Elephant Pavilion at Regent's Park Zoo, where incidentally Jean Shrimpton had already been photographed by the *Sunday Times* to highlight all that was exciting and novel in design. She was wearing a Foale and Tuffin corduroy skirt suit; the building was by architects Casson, Conder & Partners.

This assertive, brutalist architecture also included Centrepoint, designed by Richard Seifert, and the Post Office Tower, opened to the public in 1966, which featured in the comedy movie *Smashing Time* (another rags-to-rich-life tale of two liberated 'dolly birds', played by Lynne Redgrave and Rita Tushingham, in search of fame, fortune and fashion). These buildings inspired a sense of innovation and modernity, and more importantly encouraged experimentation with new materials, be it concrete or plastic, architecture or fashion. The newness of technology combined with the pop art sensibility that had been brewing since the mid-1950s, and the electrifying experimental op art of Bridget Riley and Josef Albers would encourage the girls towards a new way of looking at things.

At this time art, fashion and lifestyle began to blur around the edges and all of a sudden it didn't matter whether it was the dress you were wearing, the flat you lived in, or the glass you drank from; it was all about The Look. More importantly it was the Mod Look. In January 1965 the *Evening Standard* featured model Jan de Souza wearing a black and white chequerboard trouser suit by the duo. The editorial reported that Foale and Tuffin were Mod heroes. 'Mods like their fashion on the young side, racy, fast-changing, a bit absurd if necessary and not necessarily either pretty, flattering or wearable.' This informed a set of key values that would soon provide a shock for the fashion establishment, while offering a template for the future. It is relevant to note that later that year a jejune-looking 23-year-old called Ossie Clark graduated from the Royal College to rave reviews with a collection that featured black and white, op art inspired designs.

The 1960s was a period of pure entrepreneurial chutzpah. While many believe that the 'slashy' – the freewheeling career opportunist, the model/designer/artist/DJ/club-runner/retailer – is a product of the contemporary landscape, the serial careerist (although unlabelled) was very much alive and well and making a living in Swinging Sixties London. Like the suns in a sparkling solar system, Foale and Tuffin were surrounded by a slew of creative satellites, products of a new meritocracy, who could turn their hand to whatever role they fancied. There was May Routh – sometime model/illustrator/shop manager and later costume designer; Pauline Boty – artist/model/actress; Boty's one-time boyfriend, David Cripps – a London College Of Printing photography student who designed Foale and Tuffin's striking red, white and blue logo and did assignments for the *Observer*. Probably the most outrageously opportunistic, even if accidentally so, was the magnificent James Wedge, who went from milliner extraordinaire to become an integral player on the emerging scene as owner of two of the capital's most 'happening' boutiques (Top Gear and Countdown) before picking up a camera to capture the era, its changing fashions and faces, with an insider's understanding and perspective. A small part of this hugely creative output is catalogued on the following pages. Friendship and humour in equal amounts made up the recipe for these successful entrepreneurial sorties, along with a dash of good old-fashioned innocence.

Fuelled by opportunity, this whirlpool of talented young people was egged on to explore new territories by the new media that was exploding into colour. The first colour supplement magazine accompanied the *Sunday Times* newspaper in February 1962; this was joined by the *Telegraph* in 1964 and the *Observer* a year later. *Queen* magazine had undergone a stylish rejuvenation and the newly launched *Nova* magazine had a crystal-clear agenda: to push the boundaries of publishing. These periodicals, and the existing daily news media hungry to capture the nascent youth market, were peopled by a new breed of fashion editors such as Marit Allen, Caterine Milinaire, Sandy Boler, Barbara Griggs, Meriel McCooey, Brigid Keenan, Felicity Green, Caroline Baker, Lesley Ebbetts and Molly Parkin. Bright young things interested in bright new things to wear, they were friends of the fashion folk they propelled to stardom and as much

part of the scene they recorded. With their youthful looks and the arrogance that went with it, inevitably Marion and Sally soon became the darlings of the press. On 9 November 1962 they were featured in the *Daily Mirror* under the headline 'The Young Designers'.

'It couldn't have happened at any other time but the present. A couple of students, looking too young to be taken seriously, finish their fashion design training and set up their own business … within a few months they are established as part of the new wave of young designers surging into the fashion world. … The secret of their success? They are all on the same young and light-hearted wavelength as the young and light-hearted girls who buy their clothes. Let's call them 'kooky' clothes for want of a better word.'

It seemed to Foale and Tuffin that the rest of the world was so square.

British *Vogue* was certainly struggling with the changing times. Bizarrely, while the January 1960 edition of the fashion journal championed 'changes ranging from the titanic to the trivial' (these included the Space Race, protest theatre, Velcro, white, and grand-scale fake jewellery), the accompanying editorial promoted 'The Worldly Look'.

'What's got to go is the idea that a Bardot hair-do, gamine charm and ingénue look are in tune with 1960 fashion. … Look at these pages. … Elegant, sophisticated, above all adult.'

Of course, *Vogue's* elegantly turned-out editors were fighting a losing battle and by the April 1960 edition, the cover lines said it all: 'Young ideas, Young looks, Young voices.' Incidentally, the Young Jaeger department opened to much fanfare on 1 April. 'Individuality – that's the keynote here' trumpeted one headline. In the same issue an 18-year-old Grace Coddington (the winner of the Vogue Young Idea Model Contest) wore girlie gingham checks, just like Bardot.

By April 1962 a fashion story called *Young Idea Goes West*, showing model Jean Shrimpton photographed on the streets of New York by David Bailey, would help change the direction of fashion forever. The combination of these three made for electrifying photographs that were almost reportage in style. They reflected perfectly the way in which real young people moved about the city, whether hanging out in Chinatown, prowling down Third Avenue to discover antique shops, sleazy restaurants or an Irish pub, digging the jazz at nightclubs in Harlem or The Maisonette in the basement of the St Regis Hotel, or just checking out the latest craze in the Big Apple – public telephone booths. It is noteworthy that at this time, with silver grey swirling lacquered hair intact, *Vogue's* elegant matriarch Mrs Exeter still appeared modelling within the pages of the magazine.

Another *Vogue* editorial that would have a momentous upshot for the Foale and Tuffin duo was a show-stopping fourteen-page feature that appeared on the Young Idea pages in September 1961. Titled 'How to be a hit when you're a Miss' the pages featured the Knightsbridge Woollands department store, or more specifically its new 21 Shop (referred to in the story as the '21 Room'), which promised to feature fresh new young fashions that were 'simple, zany, not for squares (in any sense)'. Once again photographed by upstart lensman David Bailey, alongside the models in the photo shoot were virile young men, all brilliant, palpable hits in their fields, including drama critic Kenneth Tynan, entertainer George Melly, racing driver Stirling Moss, hairdresser Vidal Sassoon, photographer Terence Donovan and comedian Peter Cook. There was also The Temperance Seven, actually nine young jazz musicians born out of the RCA, who would play at a fashion show staged by 'Young Idea' for the opening of the 21 Shop on 14 September.

The brainchild of Woollands MD Martin Moss, the 21 Shop experience was a new style of shopping that would be quickly copied by the 'maiden aunt' department stores – Miss Selfridge was launched as an independent store in 1966, while 1967 saw the opening of Harrods Way In, a shop-within-a-shop.

In an issue of *Vogue* from earlier that month, an advertisement for the Harvey Nichols department store offering 'The Knightsbridge Look' couldn't have presented a more opposite guise with a model wearing a bell-shaped tweed coat with gloves and flowerpot beaver hat that were a throwback to 1950s modishness and decorum. The fashion pages that followed showed the Look In London and featured fashion houses such as Cavanagh, Ronald Paterson, Michael, Hardy Amies, Victor Stiebel and Lachasse. This was not the London that Foale and Tuffin wanted any part of.

Foale and Tuffin's breakthrough moment was as simple as the grey frill-front shift dress that precipitated it: 'This is the dress that was bought by Woollands 21 Shop, spotted by *Vogue* magazine and sold seventy copies in a few weeks. It cost ten and a half guineas.' It appeared on the pages of *Vogue* on 1 March 1962.

It was Vanessa Denza, the 18-year-old buyer for the Woollands 21 Shop, that couldn't get enough of Foale and Tuffin's designs. An order for two or three dresses might sell out on the way to the hanging rail, not even making it to the windows, and by the afternoon would be reordered in the hundreds and sometimes thousands. As Denza encouraged more young talent, across London makeshift bed-sit workrooms became design studios, and (professional or otherwise) it was a short step on to teams of sewing machinists, outworkers and factories.

Denza organised for Foale and Tuffin to design for the new Sindy doll, who first appeared in September 1963, launched by Pedigree Dolls and Toys, wearing her 'Weekenders' outfit – a patriotic red, white and blue striped top, jeans, beatnik-style duffel coat and white plastic trainers. 'Sindy is the free, swinging girl that every little girl longs to be,' read the doll's publicity. 'Every genuine Sindy outfit is a child's dream come true. Each one is designed for today's fashionable young woman by today's leading women designers. They are authentic miniature replicas of the latest adults' clothes.'

Sindy represented the new fashion look perfectly. She was the ultimate liberated 'dolly bird'. However, her real life counterparts were perhaps not quite as unshackled as they might like to think. In the fashion press women were often depicted as vulnerable, passive and baby-faced with wide-eyed fake lashes. Heads were emphasised and enlarged by the fashion photography of the time, which also accentuated a gawky, bendy-legged stance. 'Girls dressed to look under the age of consent', said Mary Quant.

When Foale and Tuffin moved into their showroom in Ganton Street the teenage Jenny Boyd became their house model. Boyd was the sister of model Pattie (herself wife of Beatle George Harrison) and the supposed inspiration for 'Jennifer Juniper' by pop singer Donovan, whom she dated. In 1965 the *Evening Standard* profiled

Jenny. 'For the rest of her life she will know exactly what she wants to wear and what, of all that's IN, most suits her – whether it's trouser suits or fluffy chick dresses or vamp clothes or cowboy kit. She and her generation, are the headache, the mainstay, and the future of the whole fashion whirl of this country.'

During the first half of the decade there was a definite change in perspective. All of a sudden there was a scene to be part of, albeit small and fundamentally London-centric. That scene was all about inventiveness, a certain naivety and experimentation. It was uniquely British in its amateurish approach, as acknowledged warmly by many of the contributors to this book. Unaware of the existence of wholesale suppliers, a lot of the fledgling designers often ended up buying their fabrics over the counter from big department stores. Foale and Tuffin used Liberty fabrics as much for their look as for the fact that the store was 'just around the corner, so handy'. Mary Quant bought many of the fabrics for her original designs from Harrods, 'because they gave good tick'. This half-baked innocence has continued to inform the British fashion industry until the present day, no matter how professional the business may have become or how professionally it has been portrayed. It has also inspired the best of our visionary fashion designers to venture where the clued-up and more calculating might fear to tread.

Foale and Tuffin symbolised that same fearlessness which has helped shape British fashion and which would soon become a blaring 'do your own thing' rally call. The real shift was that this new breed (as identified by Conran in his own contribution to this book) no longer wanted to emulate Parisian chic. Instead they created their own approximation of 'well-dressed', which was not to look as if you were trying too hard, or, as Foale and Tuffin call it, 'dressing down'. In contemporary vernacular, it was the birth of *cool*. Not for nothing were the young British women inspired by the streets of Paris, especially the Left Bank. They were excited by Juliette Gréco, the new beatnik styles, French *Elle* magazine (a fundamental inspiration cited by both Pauline Smith and Barbara Hulanicki – Foale and Tuffin were over the moon when their clothes were featured on its cover) and the nouvelle fashion designers making a name for themselves on the other side of the Channel, such as the Gauloise-thin and bespectacled Emmanuelle Khanh and later the Gauloise-thin and flame-haired Sonia Rykiel.

If low on ideas, 'we take a trip to Paris – those Left Bank girls have some super ideas,' Marion Foale once told a reporter.

Foale and Tuffin joined the queue of Europhiles who looked to the Continent – specifically France and Scandinavia – for the last word in clean, modern, 'with-it' design. 'With it!' became the watchwords for contemporary culture. While the international press raved about this new-fangled pop sensibility and featured the best of British designers that were transforming the landscape (always with a Union Jack somewhere in the vicinity), young people would make the pilgrimage from all over the UK, Europe and beyond, just to shop at boutiques in Carnaby Street and the Kings Road.

Things happened quickly for Foale and Tuffin and their circle of friends, who were at the epicentre of a new generation. Even American *Vogue*, under the auspices of the flamboyant fashion doyenne Diana Vreeland, was suddenly sitting up and taking notice of the British movers and shakers. In 1963 Vreeland famously proclaimed 'The British are coming' and by the middle of the decade the likes of Julie Christie, Rita Tushingham, Michael Caine and David Hockney were among the new breed of British exports that regularly appeared between the pages of the magazine. Hairdresser Vidal Sassoon was a favourite, and not just the man himself; his wigs got their own write-ups: 'Sassoon's wigs spent their evenings being rushed around Paris by taxi and by messengers or motorbikes. There wasn't a mannequin who didn't want to try them on; a publication that didn't want to take their pictures.'

In the 15 August 1965 edition of American *Vogue*, tucked away on the bottom right hand corner of its 'Boutique' page, was a tiny editorial. Foale and Tuffin's even tinier Marlborough Court store was big news: 'big as the top of a desk; all red, white and blue including the light bulbs in sockets ringing the ceiling. Little Misses Tuffin and Foale wait on you personally; record player going; in one of the two miniature dressing rooms, an adorable Mod, doing the jerk while trying on jeans …' Just below followed a mention of James Wedge billed as 'Hatter to the London Young'.

Perhaps one of the most important sea changes was that these boutiques soon became hangouts in themselves as much as nightclubs like the Ad-Lib, Establishment Club and Sibylla's, the Picasso cafe or the Markham Arms pub.

From Mary Quant's Bazaar in the Kings Road to John Stephen's men's boutiques that were dotted along Carnaby Street, the ambience was as crucial as the crazy designs on sale. In a masterstroke of marketing, Stephen's emporiums, Mod Male, Male W1 and His Clothes among them, each had their own decor and musical soundtrack. One journalist described how they were indeed 'like a club – the assistants just smoke and lean against the wall and put records on'.

'Carnaby Street itself was like a club,' remembers model Jenny Boyd.

So, inspired by Quant's Bazaar, and in the slipstream of Foale and Tuffin's new boutique off Carnaby Street, new fashion shops opened up all over the capital. Barbara Hulanicki, who previously illustrated for *Queen* magazine, opened the legendary Biba in 1964 in Abingdon Road, the same year that saw Jeff Banks open Clobber and James Wedge and model Pat Booth open Top Gear and Countdown. In 1965 Pauline Fordham opened Palisades just along the street from Foale and Tuffin's workroom in Ganton Street, backed by Michael White, David Hockney and Clive Goodwin; Derek Boshier designed the signage. Zandra Rhodes and Sylvia Ayton collaborated to start up The Fulham Road Clothes Shop.

In 1966 Yves Saint Laurent followed suit, unveiling his Rive Gauche boutique in Paris, while other incarnations in London included Hung On You, the psychedelic Granny Takes A Trip, and Lee Bender's Bus Stop.

Boutique culture was a reflection of the times – ephemeral, ever-changing and in many instances inevitably short-lived. The Beatles' Apple boutique that opened (and closed) in 1968 lasted less than a year.

On the other side of the Atlantic the reverberations of 'Swinging London' were being felt. 'They called our designs Beatle clothes,' says Sally Tuffin. The *New York Times* summed it up as the 'Yeah-Yeah Beat of British Rings on Seventh Avenue'. Enter Paul Young, a businessman who understood early on the connection between young people, music and fashion; he became a driving force for change in how America shopped and dressed. Young originally worked for J.C. Penney but it was Carl Rosen, CEO of Puritan Fashions Corporation, a fashion manufacturer on Seventh Avenue, who took the risk when he authorised Young to create a division of Puritan called Youthquake in 1965.

Young helped propel the British fashion pack to international stardom when he travelled to London and handpicked a small number of 'happening' designers to showcase in New York. November of that year saw the opening of Paraphernalia, a flagship store for Puritan on the corner of 67th and Madison. Its sleek space-ship style look, all curved steel, chrome and white walls, was designed by Ulrich Franzen and was the perfect setting for the far-out British fashions by Foale and Tuffin, Quant, Rhodes and Ayton alongside the latest home grown sensation Betsey Johnson. Unlike any other store, Paraphernalia would often stay open till midnight and there was always a party atmosphere. On the opening night Susannah York did the honours and Marisa Berenson walked the runway. American *Vogue* wrote: 'There were the prettiest girls; the best dancers; the super New York swingers; the police (smiling) – and later on Senator Edward M. Kennedy.' Another entrepreneurial friend of Foale and Tuffin, John Jesse, (part antiques dealer, part designer) was pictured dancing. His 'dizzy' op art shirt and tie was available in store 'in sizes for men and women'.

In a later edition of American *Vogue* Jean Shrimpton was photographed modelling her own line of clothes. 'British, individual, smashing' and available at Paraphernalia.

What Foale and Tuffin had throughout their career was the ability to tap into the right mood of the moment. They possessed that indefinable, almost chimerical quality that any would-be fashion designer needs if they are going to succeed, a kind of sixth-sense that was continually referred to in press reports about the duo. Call it sartorial extrasensory perception.

"We went to Spain for a fortnight – lay on the beach and thought about epaulettes. We went crazy for them!" said Marion.

While not intentionally calculated, their 'kooky' style created an off beat profile for the pair. This was best encapsulated by their fabric choices, from nun's veiling to the Liberty prints previously the domain of nannies and their charges (telling, perhaps, as the look of the day not only offered young women the chance to dress in a youthful style but often rolled back the years from teenage to positively childlike proportions). Even their use of flannel and corduroy was seen as unusual, let alone the underwear satin that provoked outrage (mock or otherwise) from the *Daily Mail* headline writers. 'Slinky! Sleazy! IF AT FIRST YOU THINK SHE'S ALL GOT UP IN JUST A SLIP READ ON.'

In a 'Make Yourself a Sand Shift' feature the girls suggested using Swedish furnishing cotton ('in prune with yellow, orange and blue') or black and white tablecloth gingham ('it's pretty and it's inexpensive'). Another do-it-yourself skirt was made from old-fashioned bedspread candlewick lace – 'the latest rage!'

"We were drawn to it because it was different," says Marion. "We were going to be different".

"I think we were drawn to being contrary," says Sally.

Foale and Tuffin were always at the forefront of new ideas and experimentation, reflecting the artists of the day. It was this challenging of the perceptions of the day that would soon lead to the likes of women's lib, gay lib, black power, and all manner of political and social unrest that culminated in the worldwide student riots of 1968.

It was not only the clothes, filled with humour and, more often than not, a few well-placed holes (as James Wedge remembers of a trouser suit worn by Jane Birkin) that bucked convention. The duo themselves happily faced up to the run-ins with fabric salesmen and grey-suited bank managers who regularly would ask to see the man in charge, or the publican who refused to sell them their favourite tipple. One article at the time notes a Campari and soda for Sally and a brandy and ginger for Marion.

Further emphasising the pair's blatant disregard for convention was the fact that the look and the production were, for the most part, non-seasonal. During the same period Mary Quant is reported to have been making up to twenty-eight collections a year. At Foale and Tuffin the ideas were flowing equally fast. In the *Sunday Times* in October 1964 fashion writer Brigid Keenan identified Russian inspired fashion in a story called 'Only A Steppe

Away'. By now Foale and Tuffin were offering cut velvet, frog-fastened, hemmed and collared in fake astrakhan, a ribbed sweater and an astrakhan pill box. A week later in the same publication the pair, who 'have just got home from the States – personal appearances, feted like film stars with rave reviews of their clothes in the press', were offering 'a short sleeved sweater dress in sherbet pink knitted cotton edged in pink crochet.'

Their inventiveness saw an outpouring of ideas that were both PR savvy and practical in their design, often at the same time. In 1966, two decades before Donna Karan made her career based on the idea, Foale and Tuffin presented the world with 'The Body' – an all-in-one leotard-style garment. 'The secret of why the top stays put' was revealed by Felicity Green in the *Daily Mirror*, which pictured a model wearing a see-through miniskirt, 'hurriedly made from polythene and masking tape to give an X-ray view …'

Green rightly acknowledged the duo's new status: 'one of the brightest, buzzingest fashion teams who have a flourishing export business, a wholesale manufacturing business and a shop off Carnaby Street.'

While 'who produced the first trouser suit?' is one of those questions that fashion historians continue to debate, it soon became a symbol of liberation, and for hip teenage girls like Jenny Boyd it was 'marvellous: the most logical, convenient super around-town-and-country wear anyone ever dreamed up.' Another practical solution. In October 1965 in the *Evening Standard*, Boyd models an 'immensely sober sludge-coloured wool' trouser suit by Foale and Tuffin. 'You can buy it, a month from now – the production line sold right out the minute it was issued – at Woollands 21 Shop.'

The following year the *Daily Mail* noted that 'Girls Will Be Boys'. 'Like it or not – and many men don't – trouser suits for girls are here to stay.' They highlighted the number of trouser suits in the latest collections of Foale and Tuffin and Gerald McCann and did their own bit of Union Jack waving. 'All these designers were on the same wavelength as Courrèges and produced their first trouser suits for Summer '64.'

The link between fashion and music is inextricable, and especially idiosyncratic in relation to the British scene. In the 1960s the influence and inspiration of a TV programme like *Ready Steady Go!* must be acknowledged and should not be underestimated at a time when this was the one chance for young people up and down the length of Britain to access the emerging pop scene in their own living rooms, much to the disapproval of their tut-tutting parents. The pop show that debuted on air in 1964 offered a host of new role models for young women, not least presenter Cathy McGowan, who was seen as Queen of the Mod scene along with performers such as Lulu, Cilla Black, Marianne Faithfull and Sandie Shaw.

Foale and Tuffin have often been referred to in the same breath as The Beatles, and their journeys followed the same route, note for note, seam for seam. In 1962 The Beatles released their first single 'Love Me Do', a gauche nursery rhyme-style love song that perfectly suited their boyish 'mop-tops' and clean-cut 'Sunday best' appearance. Meanwhile Foale and Tuffin dressed their girlfriends and a legion of 'wannabes' in cute little-girl shift dresses. By 1968 The Beatles had dropped out, discovered Eastern mysticism and flower power and recorded 'Revolution'. With this mood of unrest and counter-revolution, and with 'psychedelia' hanging heavy in the air, Foale and Tuffin were inspired to produce a hallucinatory swirl of paisleys, kaftans, frills, milkmaid smocks and oriental silhouettes.

In the same year the cover of *Nova* magazine summed up the feeling of confusion specifically facing young women in society. 'I have taken the pill. I have hoisted my skirts to my thighs, dropped them to my ankles, rebelled at university, abused the American Embassy, lived with two men, married one, earned my keep, kept my identity and, frankly … I'm lost'.

As society fragmented and splintered, likewise fashion was searching for a direction. It did what fashion always does when it can't see a clear way forward, it looked to escape into fantasy worlds and far-off cultures, nostalgia and ethnicity. Art deco, art nouveau, Aubrey Beardsley and Victoriana offered a little romance while Woodstock, *Hair* and the hippy trail ushered in a mood of de luxe Bohemia.

By 1971 *Vogue* magazine was presenting 'A multiplicity of summers' which appeared on the pages as a confusion of prints ranging from Boldini elegance to pointillist scrolls. There were meadows of flowers, an ebb

Contact sheet for photo session
featuring Marion (right) and Sally,
1967, *James Wedge.*

and flow of pattern, garlanded, stencilled and bordered in a drift of frenetic floral designs. Also in *Vogue*, Talitha Getty, heiress and poster-girl for the 'Beautiful People', posed in the latest collection of quilted Liberty print designs by Foale and Tuffin. On Getty the layered outfits took on a distinctly Russian folkloric peasant look. A few pages further on in the magazine actress Audrey Hepburn posed in a silky flowered midi dress, this time by Foale and Tuffin's hero, Hubert de Givenchy. By the summer, versions of Foale and Tuffin's floral print smocks were appearing everywhere from Bus Stop to Peter Robinson.

An issue or two later and the mood had turned even more fanciful, with 'delightful bright thoughts of finery' from Pablo et Delia alongside Mister Freedom's colourful, zany dungarees, T-shirts and tights. 'From Japan via Paris' came Kenzo Takada. Against this backdrop were Foale and Tuffin's colourful clownish satins, banded in rainbow-bright colour.

And so a decade that was born with so much hope was having to grow up fast. In 1960 Kennedy was the future; by 1968 JFK, his brother Bobby and Martin Luther King, each of them politicians of the young and dispossessed, had all been assassinated. The dream was turning into a nightmare.

As the Foale and Tuffin label gasped its last breath at the start of the 1970s it was perhaps the perfect time to call it a day. At their brilliant best they personified the 'Live Fast, Die Young' slogan. Now they would be buried with a good-looking corpse. In fashion's Hall of Fame they would always be 'swinging'.

Looking back, it is plain to see that the teenage girls who would run up the latest looks for themselves with paper Simplicity and Butterick patterns in their bedrooms were not so far removed from Foale and Tuffin who took the process one step further and literally set up shop on the back of a handful of little dresses. "We made our own clothes and we realised that there was a gap," says Sally. "So it was very much that people would make their own clothes, people would dress themselves and style themselves from bits and pieces, and that was happening then and we just sort of jumped in and made the bits and pieces for them."

The 1960s was a time of big ideas and even bigger hopes and dreams. This book celebrates the dreamer and the visionary, but mostly the two bolshy, 'pint-sized' little girls who for a decade made a big impression on the British fashion scene.

Schoolgirl Sally, c.1947 (left).
Schoolgirl Marion, 1947 (right).

 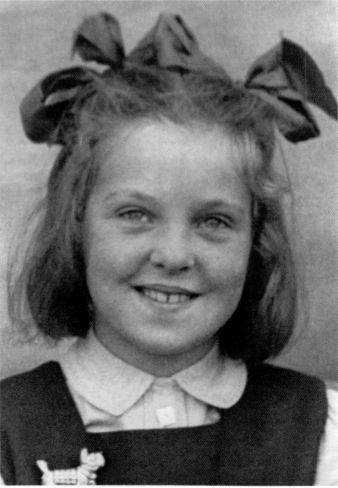

Clockwise from top:
Marion and Grampa, 1956.

Left to right: mother Gertie,
Marion and sister Christine, 1952.

Sally in Florence, 1958.

# QUITE
# AN
# EYE
# OPENER

**Foale and Tuffin conversation one**
Iain R. Webb

### Let's start at the beginning, how you met at college?

**s** / Which college?

**M** / Walthamstow. We first met there. 1955. I was sixteen.

**s** / But I was the year before you.

**M** / I know, I went when I was sixteen and I was born in 1939.

**s** / I think I did as well.

**M** / So you were already there. You'd been there for a year already, but I arrived in 1955.

### And what was the course?

**M** / Arts & Crafts. That's what it was called.

### And you went straight from school?

**s** / I went from a Quaker boarding school and Marion went …

**M** / I went from the Ilford County High School for Girls. Which I hated (both laugh).

**s** / So I said to a girl at lunchtime 'Are we allowed to go out at lunchtime?' and she looked at me as if I was absolutely bonkers.

**M** / My first day at Walthamstow I went straight up the pub because my parents had never let me go out anywhere. I'd never had a drink, nothing.

**s** / It's a good job your parents aren't alive to hear you say that (laughs).

**M** / Gosh if they knew.

**s** / The college was huge.

**M** / The South West Essex Technical College and School of Art.

**s** / And all sorts of things happened there, it was a massive building.

**M** / Well, the art school was tiny but it was a big tech with a huge hall and theatre.

**s** / So there were lots of other things to get involved with like …

**M** / There was music at lunchtime and films.

**s** / And a huge restaurant where you could get Wagon Wheels and hamburgers.

### And what did you both look like at that time?

**s** / Gorgeous!

**M** / I know exactly what I wore, on my first day I had red Capri pants, ballet shoes and I can't remember what colour the top was, but I know I also made myself a green circular felt skirt with a black dolman sleeve top and a lavatory chain belt.

**s** / We wore fifties clothes, it was very 'fifties', and it was very much Bardot.

**M** / That came later, but it was very 'fifties'.

### Very Audrey Hepburn in 'Roman Holiday'?

**s** / Yes.

**M** / At that time I used to go to the 100 Club in Oxford Street with my sister, in 1955, so we were jiving and I was listening to jazz. So you had to wear the clothes that you could dance in.

### So ponytails?

**s** / No it wasn't ponytails, it was …

**M** / No, that was later.

**s** / So what was mine like? Oh, mine was very short like Jean Seberg.

**M** / I think mine was a bit longer, I can't quite remember, and you wore black sweaters.

**s** / I thought, if you go to art school you wear a black sweater

### What did you make of each other? How did you meet?

**s** / There were about five like-minded people who went there. There was Sylvia Ayton and Jimmy Wedge.

**M** / But I was sort of an outsider because I was a year later, I went to be a painter. I didn't know fashion design even existed, but Sally had chosen fashion.

**s** / No I didn't, I went to be a painter because my dad was a printer. My father, at the end of the war because he did all the maps, he got a place in the Berlin School of Art which was magic for him, but he got pneumonia and couldn't take the place so his daughter was going to go to art school. He was determined that I went. He used to tell me how to paint and do this and do the other, so I went as a painter and when you walked in the door they said to you, 'What craft will you do 'Lino' or 'Dress'?' And I didn't know what 'Lino' meant, I hadn't got a clue, so I said 'Dress' and I'd no idea that that meant that you were channelled away from being a painter and into another field, but we did do a lot of sculpture. We had a wonderful sculpture teacher, we did wonderful still lifes.

**M** / And we did a lot of life drawing there and that taught me more than anything.

**s** / Eric Hebborn taught us that … the master forger. I've still got drawings of his; he showed you how to draw a skull. Brilliant. Brilliant.

**M** / For me the life class meant an awful lot, it was totally three-dimensional, and sculpture, and we also did composition, fine art with Margaret Green, she was very good.

**s** / And architecture.

**M** / Architecture and anatomy; very important. We had to draw a skeleton and all the muscles, and it really taught you how the body is built and how it stood up.

**s** / And Daphne Brooker made us do fashion drawing. She would bring somebody in wearing a certain dress and say, 'Right, draw this' and then the drawings were pinned on the wall and the only one who could ever do it properly was Sylvia Ayton (laughs).

**M** / She still can, she's a fantastic fashion artist.

**s** / And you had rubber plants and things to draw.

**M** / But I did 'Lino' and I only swapped to fashion because I realised that I'd got to earn a living and painting wasn't going to do it for me, and because both my parents were in the rag trade I knew exactly how to cut a pattern and make everything anyway. I thought, well I might as well do this fashion thing.

### So you were in different years?

**M** / Yes, but I skipped a year because I knew how to cut patterns already, I'd done all of that, so I didn't have to learn it.

**S** / Did they teach us pattern cutting there?

**M** / Yes, they did do pattern cutting there but I knew exactly how to make a garment from start to finish, didn't have to learn any of that.

**S** / I thought we did patterns at the Royal College

**M** / We did them there as well, oh yes. But they were much more involved at the Royal College, you worked straight onto stands, and we learnt far more at the Royal College, but they did teach us pattern cutting at Walthamstow.

### So there was a group of you?

**S** / There was a nice tight group of people who were cockney-ish.

**M** / We all came from the same sort of backgrounds.

**S** / Not smart. Not art school people really, like Jimmy Wedge was straight out of the navy. He'd just done his two years in the navy, and Sylvia was a natural rebel. You, me and there was somebody else?

**M** / I came from the most Victorian family, Victorian values.

**S** / And Mervyn and we just sort of gelled.

**M** / We did.

**S** / And the whole lot got through to the Royal College of Art.

**M** / Which is unheard of.

**S** / Because there were only ten places.

**M** / The Royal College did ask if one of them could possibly stay down a year and come back later but Daphne said, 'No, they won't do it.'

### And who was Mervyn?

**M** / Mervyn Crighton.

**S** / He looked just like Dior. He'd sit there and he was so competent, it was amazing wasn't it.

**M** / And he always wore a grey flannel suit.

**S** / He quietly got on with it and quietly did it right.

**M** / He was actually very clever at cutting and was very good, but he didn't push himself or wasn't bolshy like us lot.

**S** / He was nice; he looked after us.

**M** / We're still in touch.

### What was your day like? Where were you living?

**M** / I was made to stay at home with my parents; they refused to let me leave home so I had to come from home.

**S** / So was I. I think I was in Tottenham at that time and I used to cycle in to school.

**M** / And Sylvia lived in that terrible bedsit.

**S** / That's right. And I lived with my mother and my Irish stepfather and they were socialists, they were very, very left wing, and going to art school was the worst crime you could ever commit.

**M** / I wasn't supposed to go to art school either.

**S** / Sitting on the floor was the worst crime you could ever commit.

**M** / Why?

**S** / It was just decadent. So basically we must have both rebelled against our backgrounds.

### So it was a real shock to go to art school?

**M** / Oh, it was lovely. Wonderful. It was absolutely wonderful. My parents wouldn't let me go, my father said 'No, you can't go, you're a woman so you're just going to get married and have children and become a secretary' and I said, 'No way', so he said, 'Well, because of the money means test I've got to pay and I'm not going to.' So I said, 'OK, fine, I'll earn it', and I did. And I went.

**S** / Yes, we used to work in factories and things in the school holidays. I worked at Lovable Bras and a jeans factory. (both laugh)

**M** / Brilliant. I worked at the Army & Navy store when we were at college.

**S** / And because you were at art school you wore quite unusual clothes, so the lady in charge would take you aside and say, 'Do you think you could come in in something a bit more suitable because you are causing quite a stir'.

### And what was day to day like at college?

**S** / OK, we'd come in, what did we come in with? We'd come in with our bags of stuff. And we must have had a locker.

**M** / You'd have like one class up to break, you'd have a life class, and a lino class and …

**S** / Lunch.

**M** / Lunch, and then you'd throw water bombs out the window; go up the pub, dancing.

**S** / Evening classes.

**M** / Yes, we always did evening classes. I think that was half a ruse not to go home.

**S** / No, I think it was Daphne pushing us.

**M** / And then we'd go into the canteen in the evening and then we'd go home.

**S** / Or people would come to the hall and play like George Melly, or who was that lovely boy?

**M** / Who came from Walthamstow? Ian Dury.

**S** / So it was quite an extra-ordinary time to be part of it.

### Was it exciting to find people who loved what you loved and were excited by what you were excited by?

**S** / Yeah, I suppose it was as well.

**M** / It was a whole wonderful new world. I mean my parents didn't know such a thing as art existed. It was great! It was wonderful!

**S** / Well all I knew about art was … they did have art at the Quaker boarding school and I did a mural of the Horse Guards parade, I don't know why. Perhaps it was something to do with the coronation. Maybe? But that to me was art, and coming from that and making clothes that had little round collars, you had to wear little round collars and bits of lace round here, and puffy sleeves that you'd made in sewing class.

**m /** Very 'fifties'.

**s /** Yeah.

### So you did how many years at Walthamstow?

**s /** Four.

**m /** I did three. Two in arts & crafts and one in fashion, and everybody else did two and two.

### So when did you go to the Royal College of Art?

**m /** Well, we left in 1961. The Fashion School was in Ennismore Gardens.

**s /** It was like a real ladies' college in a beautiful house in Ennismore Gardens. Later all the Royal College Schools were housed in the new building designed by Hugh Casson built at Kensington Gore.

**m /** When you think how differently we started to dress when we went there. Janey [Ironside] was very particular.

**s /** We were sent a list where we had to go to see six theatrical performances, so many operas, you had to have done all this, and you had to go to cocktail parties. You had to wear certain shoes, certain clothes, your hair a certain way, and it harked back to Madge Garland where you had to wear a straight skirt with a split up the back. You were being trained really to be a lady.

**m /** And Janey had this daughter Virginia who would slop in with bare feet. (laughs)

**s /** So the fashion school wasn't very connected with the rest of the Royal College, because you'd meet in the common room and you'd have people like Pauline Boty, looking like God Knows What, with balloons and hair and this, that and the other, and we were much more careful about the way we dressed.

**m /** And then there was the painting school and the sculpture school, and there was David Hockney and there were all these completely different people, and we were set apart in this very sedate situation.

**s /** It was quite controlled wasn't it? And the classes were controlled.

**m /** There was a lot of teaching.

**s /** We did our classes, we did our work; it was a proper course.

**m /** And it was very well taught. We had to make absolutely everything from scratch. We had to make the pattern, do the buttonholes, you know, everything. It was absolutely brilliant.

**s /** It was good, it taught us a lot.

**m /** It taught us discipline.

### And what was the qualification at the end of the course?

**m /** It wasn't an MA.

**s /** It was meant to be an MA, it's an MA course but it was a DesRCA [Design RCA].

**m /** In fact the fashion school brought more publicity to the Royal College of Art at that time than any other course.

**s /** We were the most successful school and had a lot of publicity.

**m /** They made it into an MA, but we're actually Des RCA.

### It sounded much more formal than one imagines.

**m /** It was. I think it was pretty informal in the other schools.

### But was it still very much about ideas.

**m /** Yes, we were dead serious. We used to go to all the fashion shows in Paris like Chanel and Balenciaga, we were so into all of that, heavily into couture, but at the same time we were also heavily into what we wanted to do.

**s /** We made our own clothes and we realised that there was a gap. What was happening was that people would dress themselves and style themselves from bits and pieces and we just sort of jumped in and made the bits and pieces for them.

### Was there a line between making clothes for yourselves and what you were designing as part of college?

**m /** It was Givenchy, Chanel and what-have-you but it was with a twist. We didn't like what was being produced at that time in middle-of-the-road England, which was what we were going to have to go into. It was just not our thing at all.

### What kind of things?

**m /** Well, it was like Polly Peck and Susan Small. That was good but there weren't many openings.

**s /** There was Mary [Quant].

**m /** Yes, Mary, but it wasn't like there were openings for us out there. Mary was doing her thing, which was very impressive, and Alexander Plunkett-Green came and gave a talk at the end of our last year, and we all thought, 'Well, if they can do it, why can't we do it?' (laughs)

**s /** We just felt we didn't fit in to anything.

**m /** Well, we didn't fit in and they were able to do it.

**s /** So the only option really was to do it ourselves.

**m /** And so we were going to do it. We just were, we just weren't going to go into that middle-of-the-road, sitting in a factory.

**s /** I can't actually remember what motivated us, what we were wearing and what we were thinking at the time but we had a very busy social life. We did party a lot.

**m /** Yes, we did.

**s /** And every year we would go to France with the college and buy a pair of shoes.

**m /** Always.

**s /** We had no money and we'd go on that funny little airplane that went to Paris, and we had a route that we'd run down Rue Saint-Honoré down to the river and eventually to the Left Bank, and we knew all the best shoe shops and we would suss them all out one day and come back the next day and decide what to buy at the end.

It was really good and the shoes were very, very important.

### So at that time it was the French designers who you looked up to?

**m /** We did, we did. Their cutting.

**s /** The couturiers but not the shops.

### So, the shops were not for you?

**m /** No, not the shops. Balenciaga and Givenchy we really watched. I thought it was wonderfully cut, very clever.

**s /** I think Givenchy and Balenciaga taught us how to change from being fussy to going for pure lines and the essence of the thing.

**m /** I think they taught me about shape; about making a three dimensional, constructed look. I learnt a lot from it.

**s /** In fact, at the Royal we did have Balenciaga blocks that were used a lot.

**m /** Well, Sylvia went straight to Wallis and she used to go over to Paris and actually buy the toiles [early versions of finished garments] and bring them back and make them. That was her job.

### That was how it was; I think it was called buying the edition? The same with the America stores.

**s /** I remember seeing them hanging up in Marks & Spencer.

**m /** And now it's on the internet, you just click in and copy.

**s /** But then if you've seen a real Chanel sleeve, it is so complex and difficult to copy.

### So what sort of things were you making for yourselves at that time?

**m /** Well, I remember you making that mohair coat and you dropped a sleeve and I found it for you down Brompton Oratory. It was a 'cocoon'. We made Balenciaga 'cocoon' shapes, and then the Sack [dress]. We were into that and there was also the straight skirt phenomenon. No trousers.

s / No it was skirts, wasn't it? Straight skirts.

m / Mid-calf; quite decent for young ladies.

## Quite sophisticated before that 'Youthquake' thing happened?

m / Oh, totally. Janey [Ironside] had a look. She was always dressed in black and white with very red lips, and she'd have a white shirt and a straight black skirt and maybe a black jacket. She definitely had a look and we all kind of followed on behind. And we did a dress show at the end of our three-year course, and a degree show.

s / We did a dress show every year.

m / But the one at the end was the 'biggie'. Oh wow! I can remember some things I put in. Terrible.

s / I had a cotton lace dress that was sleeveless with a kick thing in the front and then appliquéd squares of lace, quite coarse, and I did a coat in hessian that was lined in white piqué. I can remember those two.

m / I can remember you cutting out chiffon on the cross and finding out that chiffon didn't cut on the cross. (both laugh)

s / I did a dress that was grey, maybe shantung silk or something, and quilted. No, not quilted, smocked. I smocked the band and then I put little beads on top of all the smocking. I can't remember why and I don't remember what happened to it.

m / I can't really remember what I did. I know I did something hideous and I put feathers on it and it was orange, I can remember that.

s / Oh, I did some childrenswear,

m / I did pink fluffy childrenswear.

s / A red leather coat.

## When you were working on those designs, what were your expectations of what you were going to do when you got outside college?

m / Well, there was the horror of all these ghastly places to go and work, like Susan Small, if you were lucky,

s / I didn't even think of that.

m / No, I didn't because I think we knew already that we just weren't going to do that, somehow or other.

s / You'd moved into a different world by then and you were feeling slightly elitist.

m / And you were concentrating on this collection.

s / And we had flats in South Ken[sington]. You didn't think about going back to your roots or struggling, you just sort of knew it was going to be all right. And I imagine that we were given a lot of confidence by the college system. I think they did support you amazingly; they had lots of competitions.

m / That's right – we all won things.

s / We all got awards; they managed to share them out. You just felt you could do it.

m / I think also we'd got that youth thing that we just knew that we were going to be fine, and do what we wanted to do.

s / Diana Vreeland was sweet but she thought she could … wasn't she the one who also said, 'I think it might be better if you two went off and got married'?

m / No, I think she was just pretty amazed by us, because when we went to see her in her red room we were already pretty established by then. So who was it that said we should go and get married?

s / I think it was Susan Small.

m / Susan Small. Yes.

s / And that's interesting because most women of our era did just prepare themselves for marriage.

m / And motherhood.

s / Because I was taught to cook, I was taught to sew. I was taught to be a good wife basically, which I'm not (both laugh). Our parents had come through the war.

m / They were just happy to be alive and together.

s / I think it was excusable that we were to be turned into clones really; into happy, slightly more successful clones than them.

## That thing of feeling different and not fitting in started when you were teenagers in the 1950s. Do you think that emerging from college in 1961 put a stamp on that and confirmed that you could be different?

s / Yes, you were allowed to be different in the sixties.

m / I knew I was different before I went to college because I went to this awful girls' school, and I fitted in nowhere and in no way did I fit in with my parents' lifestyle, at all. So when I was about thirteen, I just knew that's it, I don't fit in here, I'm going to do what I want to do.

s / At our diploma show after the three years at the Royal College of Art, we were in [the] same year as Hockney and he went to pick up his diploma in a gold lamé jacket, and behind the staff we all blew bubbles. So you didn't behave. But you were made to work very hard. So they taught you the work ethic. That has been invaluable.

m / It was great but we all worked really hard, we really did.

## So when you finally walked out of the doors at the Royal, what were your first thoughts? Had you decided to work together at that point?

m / Yes.

s / Yes we had.

m / To keep ourselves afloat I remember doing bridesmaid dresses for one of the fashion models of that era. Leslie Poole was doing the bride's dress and he asked me to do all the bridesmaids. So we were keeping ourselves afloat with private orders. It was just after we left, but in our own domestic situations with domestic sewing machines on the floor, that sort of thing.

s / But we used to have tea down in the basement at Ennismore Gardens and plan what we were going to do, and a fellow student, Moira O'Donnell, decided that her father had enough money to encourage us to do a collection and back us, and we all went for that. So we took our last collection with us and we offered it for sale, although I don't remember how or where we sold it. But I remember there was an article in a magazine with somebody wearing a grey sheath dress that was divided into four that we used later for something else. But it didn't work.

**M** / No, it didn't. There were too many of us. Her father was too dominant and we weren't going to be told what to do.

**S** / And we had to go all the way to Harrow on the train and we got so frustrated.

**M** / And we just didn't like being told what to do, at all. So that was not on.

**S** / So we did a moonlight flit and we took our clothes and our sewing machines back and we went to work in our flat in South Ken. Was it your flat or my flat?

**M** / Well, first of all it was in mine in Brechin Place, and then we went to Jimmy Wedge's.

**S** / No, we went to mine at one stage.

**M** / Did we? Oh yes, the Gloucester Walk one.

**S** / Yes, and then we finished up at Jimmy Wedge's, which was opposite where the Paul Smith shop is now in Westbourne Grove, and that was a restaurant at the time.

**M** / It was L'Artiste Assoiffé.

**S** / And we did most of our work on his billiard table.

**M** / The cutting out. That is when we took our first samples to Vanessa Denza at Woollands 21 Shop, and we went on top of the bus with them and she said, 'Go back and make those'. So we did our samples, and we did three of each, and we delivered them straight into the shop. Then they were in the window and Lady Rendlesham had seen it, and it was photographed, and then it was in *Vogue*, and then we had to produce thirty and we had to buy enough fabric, which was unheard of in those days because going to buy bolts of fabric was a man's thing, but we did, and then we had to cut them all out.

**S** / And make them on the billiard table.

### And that was the drawings in the pink cardboard envelope?

**M** / Yes. The grey with the frill and the red one. And that was our first *Vogue* photograph, the one with the men with all the cigarettes. It was a Bailey photograph and I don't know who the model was. She was a blonde.

### Not a bad start! (laughs)

**S** / We had no telephone so we had to walk all the way down Westbourne Grove to where Tom's Bakery is now and make a phone call at the post office. The 52 bus was our taxi, wasn't it?

**M** / Yes. We used to deliver on the bus.

### Did it all live up to your expectations?

**M** / It wasn't real.

**S** / It was good fun.

**M** / It still wasn't real but we were doing what we wanted to do.

**S** / Then that fashion artist Robb came around and drew us in his glam style and turned us into the most dreadful looking clones. He made us look all sort of …

**M** / He was a very important figure at that point, the fashion artist at the time. A lot of the time it was fashion drawing and not photography, an awful lot of it.

### The 21 Shop. Was that somewhere you went to look anyway?

**M** / It opened at a very opportune time and they were looking for things and it was suddenly just there at the right moment.

**S** / Where did we look? Oh, I know where we looked. Every Saturday we would go down the Kings Road and walk up and down and just feel what was happening, and so if somebody was wearing a snake belt suddenly it was a snake belt or denim or … it was just in the air, and you picked it up like people do now, except there weren't many people doing it.

**M** / It was street really, right from the start. It's funny isn't it?

### Were the things you were designing things you and the girls around you wanted to wear?

**M** / Yes. Yes.

**S** / Or the men. We'd make them ties, encourage them to buy certain shoes or cut their hair in a certain way, and we were all very aware of people like Vidal very early on, anyone who had a cutting edge you sort of homed in on.

**M** / And when we first bought fabric we didn't know that you could buy wholesale. (laughs)

**S** / We bought from Dickins & Jones.

**M** / And then we found out and we went to these places to buy fabric, and it was really funny because they didn't want to sell it to us. We'd want to buy a whole bolt, thirty yards, and it came in 36, 48, or 54 inches wide, but they really were absolutely gobsmacked that there was two little girls coming in to buy fabric and it wasn't a man in a grey suit. They really couldn't understand it, but in the end they let us.

**S** / When we were working at Gloucester Walk just before we did the Woollands thing, there was a pub down the road which had a quite nice saloon. And we were sitting outside ordering a drink and the publican came out and asked us how old we were, and we said, 'What do you mean how old are we, we are old enough to drink, we run a business' and he just said, 'I don't care what business you are in, you cannot drink here,' and sent us packing.

**M** / And then we went back again with our accountant and our passport and he still sent us off.

### How old were you then?

**S** / Well we had already left the Royal College, so we were twenty-one or two.

**M** / Somewhere around there.

**S** / But we didn't really look it, because – I remember being in New York and it was quite hard getting into clubs, and you had to travel with your passport because it was too much of a bore.

**M** / And we weren't wearing mumsy clothes like we were meant to be wearing, we were wearing kids' clothes, young clothes.

**S** / And you did get spat at on the street. I suppose it's a bit like when somebody first wore a bra that showed under their clothes. That must have been quite an eye-opener for people's morals.

Letter from the House of
Givenchy, Paris, 1960.

**G I V E N C H Y**

SOCIÉTÉ ANONYME AU CAPITAL DE 2.500.000 FRANCS

3, AVENUE GEORGE V - PARIS (8º)

R.C.Seine 55 B 5122  _  BAL. 92-60 À 92-62

COMPTE CHEQUE POST. PARIS 17 286 72

Paris March 3Ith, I960

Miss Sally TUFFIN
II6, Queens Gate
LONDON

Dear Miss Tuffin,

    In answer to your letter of March 28th,
we are sending you, herewith, an invitation
card for you and your friend.

    Awainting the pleasure of seing you,
we are,

            Very truly yours,

        Pour Jean Claude de GIVENCHY
        The secretary,

Sally Tuffin fitting a model
at the RCA, c.1959.

Marion models her own design,
white with pink print, in Walthamstow
Art School graduation show, 1958.

Design for a theatre or resturant suit, in silk and camel hair mixture. the jacket hangs open at the centre back, fastened at the neckline by a knot tie. the dress has a boned bodice & flying back panel.

Example of Work.

Opposite page:
Sketch for Walthamstow Art School project by Sally Tuffin, 1957.

**Top:** RCA student fashion show. Front row from left to right: Sally, Marion, Leslie Poole, model, 1962, *Drapers Record*.

**Bottom:** Styling wool coats at Selfridges: models with Sally (second from right) and Ken Sprague, c.1959.

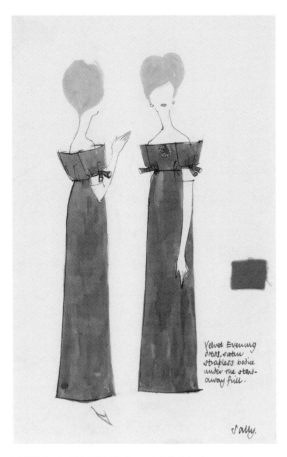

Velvet Evening
dress, satin
strapless bodice
under the stand-
away frill.

Sally.

striped towelling
beach wrap.

Sally.

Sketches for RCA project by
Sally Tuffin, c.1960.

**Opposite page:**
Sally's lace dress from RCA
diploma fashion show, 1961.

Hessian or saileloth
beach jacket

Sally.

Short evening dress
in toshers poppy print
organza, (or cotton)

Sally.

Celia Hammond modelling tweed
suit, c.1963 *Vernier*.

**Opposite page:**
Queen Elizabeth II wears Marion's
new mantle design, 1960, *Australian
Women's Weekly*.

June 29, 1960

Registered in Australia for transmission by post as a newspaper.

# The Australian WOMEN'S WEEKLY

Over 800,000 Copies
Sold Every Week

PRICE 9

**The Queen's new mantle... page 2**

**I first got to know Sally Tuffin and Marion Foale**
when we were contemporary students at
the Royal College of Art from 1959 to 1962.
I was in the painting school and they were
in the fashion school. It was an exciting and
very creative time at the Royal College, with
much interaction between the different
departments and in our social lives.

I retained contact and friendship with
them after college, when they were connected
with Carnaby Street, and we would often
meet there.

I remember their distinct designs and
their influence on fashion in the 1960s and
beyond. They always dressed well and were
a good advertisement for their designs. We
used to meet at fashion events, parties and
art openings. They added much to the lively
spirit of Britain in the 1960s.

Opposite page:
Sally (left) and Marion in workroom
at Gloucester Walk, 1962.

# Derek Boshier

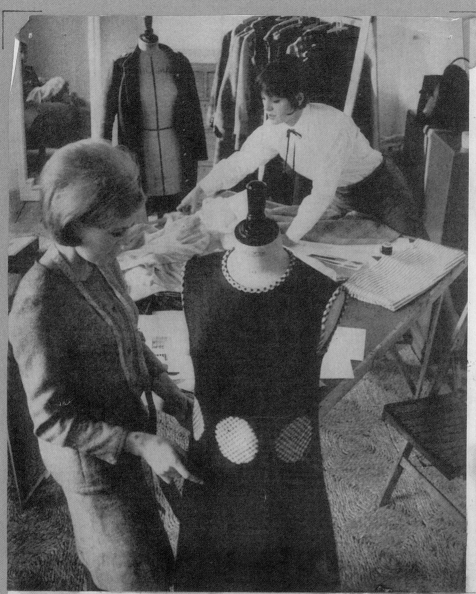

Apart from their work, which they obviously adore, they like parties and the Portobello Road. "They had a great move at college to make us read Aristotle and Socrates, but we still like pops, unfortunately." Among those uncharacteristic modern young men who step aside from the affluent trail into the

**Sally Tuffin,** *above left,* and **Marion Foale,** *above right,* have now been dress designing for about a year, and they have immediately cut out a very clear and bright image for themselves. Their ideas are young, simple, wearable, and more than with it—often before it.

Both in their early twenties, they spent four years at art school before going to the Royal College of Art. After this, starting was easy. "We just did a grey flannel dress and said 'This is it'. Woollands bought about three, and *Vogue* featured it." At first when we got orders we didn't know whether to laugh or cry because we were making everything ourselves." Woollands and Chanelle are still their chief buyers, but

they have sold a little to the USA, and also make children's clothes for "The Dolls House."

They feel that Paris is still the Mecca of fashion, but they don't look to the collections for inspiration and guidance. "We go to see what is in the shops, Galeries Lafayette, and Au Printemps, we sit in cafes and watch the young people go by, and of course we read *Elle*."

Sally Tuffin is very blonde, Marion Foale very dark, they are both tiny, alert, amusing, and speak with one voice. "No-one influences us; we influence ourselves. We only design clothes that we want to wear." They like the work of Mary Quant very much, but hate to be accused of copying. If ever they discover

that they had produced a design similar to one of hers, they drop it immediately. And of the Fashion House Group of London: "We're not really very much in touch," they said, discreetly. They seemed to be surrounded with day dresses, suits and separates, but there are one or two evening numbers: "Oh yes, we've got a right charming navy lace. We did a great long petticoat dress too."

They are certain about the future. "We are always going to be whole-sale, and sell lots at prices that people of our age can afford. That's important." Much later, they may buy a shop to sell their own merchandise, and accessories too. At the moment James Wedge occasionally designs hats for them.

**We all met at Walthamstow in the mid-1950s.**
I think I'm a bit older than the others. Sally and I were in the same year, and then Marion joined later. I think she wanted to do painting, because basically she thinks she's a painter, but she came in to do fashion at Walthamstow School of Art. Daphne Brooker, head of the Fashion Department, would say to us, 'Go to the library and get out *L'Officiel* and you'd think, 'What is she saying? What is it?', and you'd walk down the corridor, not speaking, just thinking, and you'd get to the woman in the library and just shout 'L'OFFICIEL!' And then she would show you this magazine, because then there was only *Vogue* and *Queen* I think, but *'L'Officiel'* was this big, big book full of wonderful things.

Daphne would set us a project like 'Design an organdie party dress or a fabulous dinner suit', and you'd think, 'What?' But we were all into glamour and doing wonderful big dresses. We wore tweed dirndls and flat shoes, and had our hair in ponytails, and we just loved every moment of what we were doing.

When we were at college we went to the collections. Givenchy and Balenciaga – Balenciaga was the ideal. Milliner Graham Smith was doing the hats at Lanvin so we would get to go to that show and oh, the joy. I remember when we went to the shows in Paris the Algerian war was on and everyone had guns outside, and we all got Asian flu. Daphne took us there, and she used to say that we had to go to the shops every Saturday to see what was going on.

We all graduated together. There was a group of us that would always work incredibly long hours at Walthamstow; we did evening classes everyday of the week, we learnt to draw architecture and anatomy. We just drew. Five of us tried for the RCA from Walthamstow. It was just unbelievable that we all got in; there was only twelve in the year. Each of us was into our own thing. I did tailoring quite a lot, Sally did children's wear and Marion did lots of things. Marion designed a nice outfit for the Queen, 'The Order of the British Empire'; it was a dress and cape all in one, and someone from a different department designed the hat, and others did the jewellery. We all used to have to help the third years.

When we were doing pattern cutting at RCA, we had a man called Mr Lipman and a lady called Miss Elfer who taught us toile making beautifully, and he would come up to us and say, 'This is the bust point' and we'd be like, 'Oh no, don't mention the bust point' and we'd try not to laugh. We were like silly girls.

We always had our tea and evening meal together before Marion made this long journey home to Cockfosters, and she was always coming in saying that someone had exposed themselves on the train and we would say, 'Oh no, not another one!'

I lived in Holloway with Graham David Smith, who lived with the painter and art forger Eric Hebborn, in a terrible place where you couldn't use the lavatory so you had to pee in a vase, but it was all character building. I remember we had a party and David Hockney came. It was an incredible group of people. There was always a Christmas party at the RCA, but you didn't really go to parties because your whole life was really one long party. But then when we did leave, it was like, 'Well, what do we do? Really, really, what can we do?' I always wanted to ask Daphne, what did you teach us, to make us think we could run our own businesses?

So there was Moira O'Donnell and Sandra Cormack, Sally, Marion and me, and we were going to run a business together, and I thought 'No, no, no, all these designers together is not going to work'. So I said, 'I'm not going to do it with you' and they tried to carry on and there were arguments and rows and in the end they all split up, and then it was just the two of them together. They worked with Jimmy Wedge; he had somewhere to

# Sylvia Ayton

live in Notting Hill and they moved in there with him. Jimmy Wedge was teaching at Ravensbourne and I used to teach part-time at Kingston Polytechnic, so one was always, always working.

I started making clothes for Doris Langley Moore, who started up the Costume Museum in Bath [now the Fashion Museum]. Her daughter was called Pandora and she did all these amazing paintings, and I used to go and help her there, painting three lines on the back of the mannequins hands because she never had enough gloves. Jimmy Wedge helped make the hats. Jimmy Wedge and model Pat Booth then opened Top Gear together. And another girl who used to work with Marion and Sally was Pauline Fordham, who then opened up another shop, Palisades.

I really learnt to grade patterns through Pauline Denyer, who is Mrs Paul Smith now. She was working with Marion and Sally. We were designing quite sophisticated clothes, and when it came to grading the pattern it was too hard, so everything just became a shift; really straight shapes, because I hated bust darts and because it was much easier to make. The trousers we were making were really fitted and flared; we worked really hard on them. It was quite a sexy look in a funny way. It had gone from being all about debutantes and the

like, we abandoned our bras and suspenders because you couldn't wear all that stuff under these tight clothes, and you didn't want to dress like your mother. I remember walking through Fenwick's, and the women were tutting because you were wearing a short skirt, but it wasn't really very short.

It was all happening at the same time. There was the fabulous Emmanuelle Khanh, the girl that wore the big glasses in France, who did all those pointy collars and things. Just everything was narrow and tight and clean. It was wonderful.

Marion and Sally did those wonderful 'underpant' dresses, like your Y-fronts; very different. I've got a swimming costume they did in navy towelling. They were always finding fabrics that nobody had used before, like nobody was using lace unless it was a wedding dress.

Zandra [Rhodes] would do all these wonderful designs based on medals, so she'd draw them all out and go in to show Marion and Sally, and she'd cut a hole in the middle of her paper design and put it over her head and say, 'what d'you think of this?' Marion and Sally were selling to Paraphernalia in New York. When the fabric arrived the print was sometimes smudged and they'd say, 'Sorry Zandra but we can't use this,' and she'd say

But you can cut around it,' and they'd say, 'we can't because it's expensive. The man from the shop in New York said the customers don't want these smudgy bits. It's all very well being young trendy designers, but they want something without smudges.' And then Zandra and I started doing things together.

You didn't think about things that much, you just drew it and then you just made the samples. You just wanted to make it up really quickly to see what it looked like. I don't know where Sally and Marion's factories were, but I remember going on the tube to Bounds Green, because we didn't have a car, with patterns and fabric flying everywhere, and going into the factory. And everybody would look at you, and Zandra looked even stranger than me, and you would have to try to explain to them how you wanted it made. When the stuff arrived you had to pack it into boxes and send it by Red Star off to wherever, or take it round to the shops yourself, knock on the door and say, 'Can we be paid?'

Bridal designs by Marion.
Left to right: bride Jackie Browne
and bridesmaid Marion,1955.

Sally (right) with Sylvia Ayton,
graduating from the RCA,1961.

**Opposite page:**
Mary Murray Model Modes
Ltd: (from left to right) Marion
Foale, Sally Tuffin, model, Moira
O'Donnell, Sandra Cormack,
1961, *Sunday Times/Fashion
Museum, Bath.*

Dress in scarlet
doctor flannel
with magenta
felt looped
ruffle.

Foale and Tuffin sketches for
first collection including grey
flannel frill dress, shown in pink
cardboard envelope, 1962.

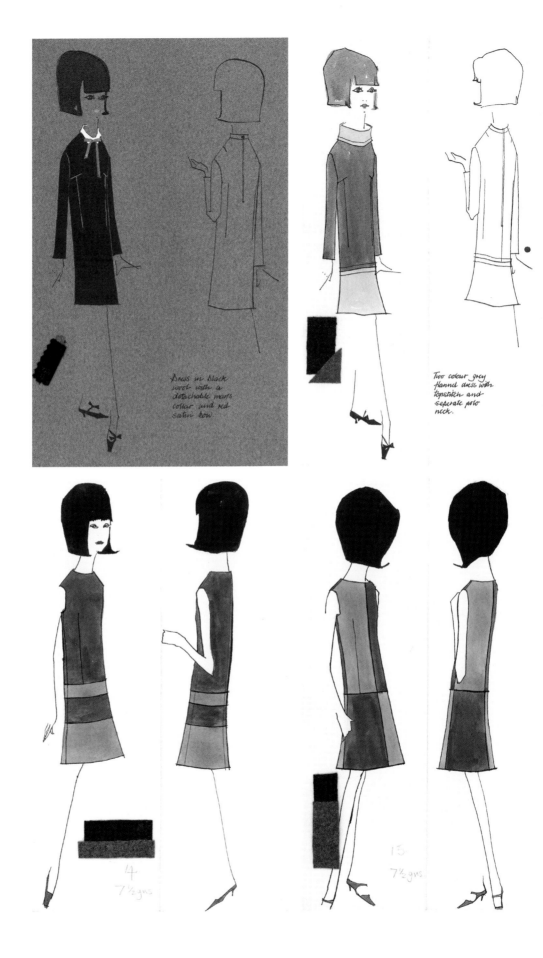

Dress in black
wool with a
detachable mans
collar and red
satin bow

Two colour grey
flannel dress with
topstitch and
seperate polo
neck.

4
7½ gns

5
7½ gns

Two colour grey
flannel dress
with white
binding.

Foale and Tuffin sketch for
grey flannel frill dress, 1962.

**Opposite page:**
Grey frill front dress, 1962,
*David Bailey/Vogue* © *The Condé
Nast Publications Ltd.*

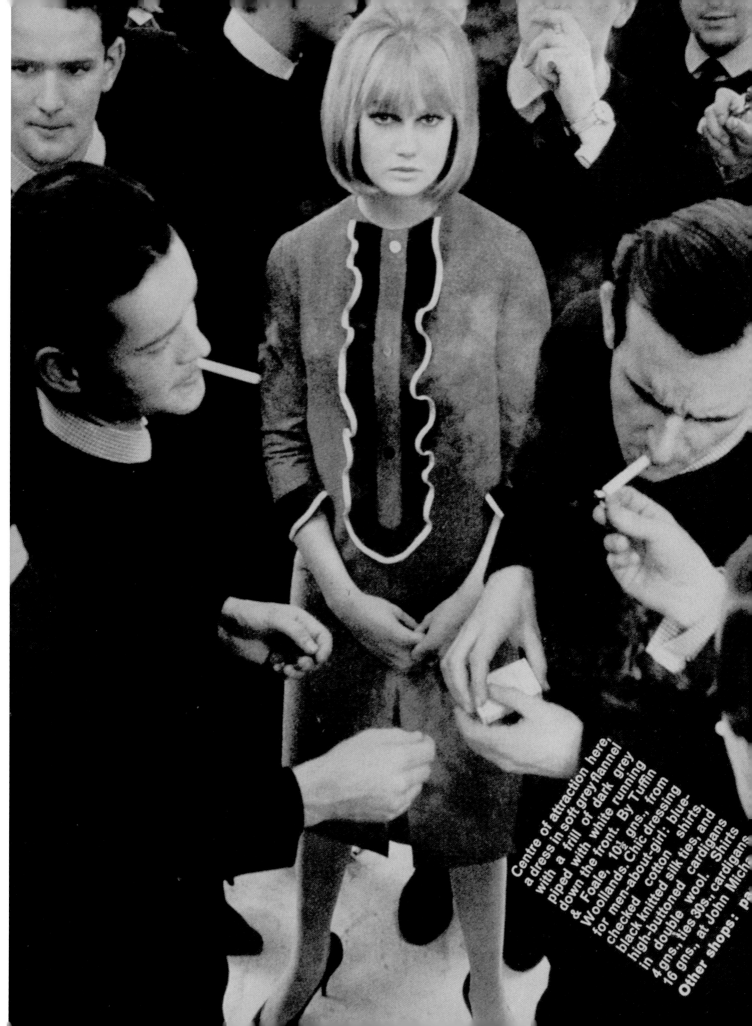

Centre of attraction here, a dress in soft greyflannel with a frill of dark grey piped with white running down the front. By Tuffin & Foale, 10½ gns., from Woollands. Chic dressing for men-about-girl: blue-checked cotton shirts, black knitted silk ties, and high-buttoned cardigans in double wool. Shirts 4 gns., ties 30s., cardigans 16 gns., at John Michael. Other shops: pa

# DESIGNERS

*Robb* REPORTS ON TWO

TALENTED NEWCOMERS

TO THE FASHION WORLD

LET me introduce you to two clever young designers: Marion Foal, aged 23—pictured on the right in my fashion workshop sketch—and Sally Tuffin, 24.

Now look at the smart, low-backed black and white cocktail dress on this side of the page . . . I spotted it at a recent fashion show, asked to meet the designer, and found that there were, in fact, *two* designers: Marion and Sally, working together.

My big drawing shows them as I found them, hard at work in their workroom in Notting Hill, London, surrounded by their sketches, patterns and materials.

Alongside, I've sketched some of the bright fashion ideas I picked up from my visit to their studio.

At first, I thought Marion and Sally were just a couple of crazy cats (hep variety) having fun. But I soon realised what intelligent, serious-minded career girls they are . . . and how good at their jobs.

It took five years of hard work at the Royal College of Art Fashion School, in London, to teach them all they know. Now, with their fingers very much on the pulse of fashion, they are at work on their own, producing designs for important stores like Woollands, Harrods and Peter Jones.

Their designs are like themselves—young, casual and colourful. But as simplicity's the keynote, their clothes are also chic and copyable.

## Paris influence

Originality in everything is the girls' aim, but they don't hesitate to pick up ideas on their frequent trips to Paris. Here, are some of their fashion tips.

● HAIRSTYLES: Longer, but styled, with a black bow for evening wear. For parties, blonde Sally favours a style started by Carita—a top-knot drawn into an elastic band and decorated with a velvet bow. Marion wears her shoulder-length hair in a French twist. Both agree that the new, longer hair is easier to manage.

● SHOES: Lightweight, definitely strappy. The girls get theirs from Paris, but you can find almost exact replicas in the shops here now. (Incidentally, don't forget to buy heel-less, seamless, toeless stockings if you want the barefoot look).

● PARTY DRESSES: Backless for the young sophisticate. That's obvious from the stunning cocktail dress pictured, which, incidentally, I saw made up in Sophistic—the first knitted rayon to be washable and completely stable, with a crease-resistant finish.

Easy to copy, this *could* be your last year's party dress with the back cut right down to the waist, the hem and waist bedazzled with black rick-rack braid.

● CRAZY JEWELLERY: Smart idea for the young . . . medals worn as brooches. Sally and Marion bought theirs (see main sketch) in London's Portobello-road. But you could try borrowing father's or grandfather's old war medals.

● MATERIALS: The girls favour woollens, large and small checks, and lots of gingham and denim. Marion and Sally design coats in grey and blue denim, stitched with white.

*Idea to copy:* A denim pinafore dress with a bright check shirt (see sketch). It's the little-boy-grown-up look.

Marion and Sally are certainly with-it. Their clothes have a gaiety and distinctive style that's sure to sell. I predict an equally bright future for them.

*Fashion problems?
Write to: Woman's
Mirror Fashion Dept.,
Fleetway House,
Farringdon-st.,
London, E.C.4.*

AUGUST 18, 1962

*NEXT WEEK: Woman's Mirror takes you to the Royal College of Art Fashion School, where these two young designers were trained, to meet the students who will be the designers of the future. And for 1s. 6d. we'll be offering a prize-winning design by a talented student: the pattern for a fabulous four-piece autumn outfit, specially designed for Woman's Mirror.*

Woollands advertisement featuring
yellow wool coat, 1964.

**Opposite page:**
21 Shop advertising featuring
Celia Hammond (left) and Jean
Shrimpton (right) modelling Varuna
wool Liberty print dresses, 1963.

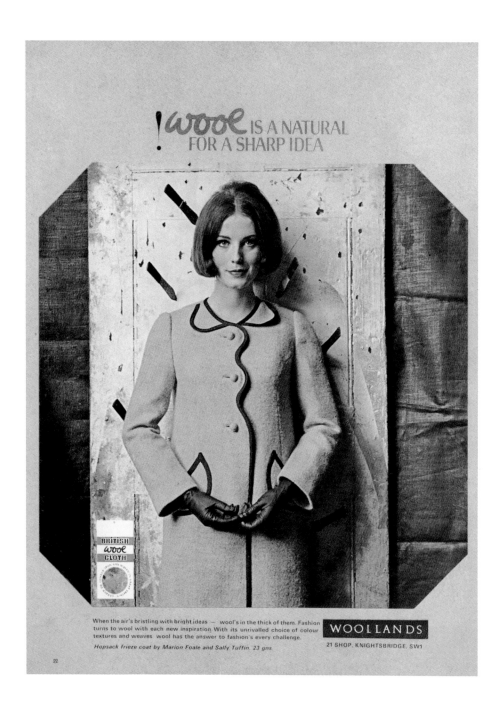

# 21
## shop

*Everyone's getting into print this season*

at any time,
any place.
Fine wool in
four colour ways.

Sizes 8 to 14
Suit £16.16.0
Dress £11.15.0

**WOOLLANDS**
Knightsbridge · SW1

**MARSHALL
AND SNELGROVE**
Oxford Street · W1
and BIRMINGHAM

**When I was 18 years old everybody's thing** was to become a secretary. I decided I didn't want to go that route so I went over to Paris and went to see *Vogue*, but they said my typing skills were ridiculous so they shipped me off to Jacques Fath and from there I went to Galleries Lafayette, where I started to learn about buying. I realised that was what I wanted to do, so I came back to England and went to Woollands and met Martin Moss (the husband of photographer Jane Bown) who was the architect of a new department store style.

One day Moss announced that he wanted to open the 21 Shop at Woollands and he wanted me to be one of the buyers. The whole idea of the 21 Shop was to make clothes for young people, because back then there was only Mary Quant and Kiki Byrne. Nobody made size eights or tens apart from Jaeger, and girls were wearing white gloves on the tube. I used to make my own clothes and people would come up and ask if they could buy my clothes but I never wanted to be a designer, I realised my forte was picking.

The whole project was on the ground floor so people could come straight in opposite Harvey Nichols. Terence Conran was brought in to design the 21 Shop and Claire Rendlesham was appointed the equivalent of creative director; she was of course 'Young Ideas' director of *Vogue*.

At the start we had to strong-arm manufacturers to do what we wanted because nobody really believed there was a market. We were working totally in the dark; you didn't know if it was going to be a success. Claire was pushing people like Susan Small. Martin brought in another buyer from Simpson's called Maggie Arkle and the two of us were given the brief to develop all this. Terence Conran's design for the shop – these were the first days of pine – was wonderful but after the first six months we had to pull it apart because it was a shoplifter's paradise. Terence was wildly furious. Nobody thought about security tags and that sort of thing because before that nobody had stocked clothes that anybody had wanted to shoplift!

We had fabulous windows. The windows were changed twice a week. Can you imagine? In September 1961 Martin hired The Temperance Seven for three shows. Nobody had music for their shows; I think Mary [Quant] had music but nobody else. The shows were at six o'clock, nine o'clock and midnight, and were staged in the department, so we had to clear all the clothes out. By the midnight show there was a queue right the way round the block trying to get in – we could have done twenty shows. Vidal [Sassoon] did the hair, and Claire did photographs with David Bailey and Jean Shrimpton to promote the event. These were big breakthroughs.

It was like a dam breaking when we started. In those days buyers had to run the department, meet the staff, do the budgets and check the sales; you had to do it all. I was twenty-two. Within three months I did the figures that I was supposed to do for a year. What was obvious was that we needed special clothes. Peter Shepherd, who was teaching at the Royal College of Art – the most brilliant hat designer, who taught James Wedge – suggested to Martin that Maggie [Shepherd] be brought in and that Maggie, who was working with Janey Ironside at the RCA, should bring in some designers from the RCA to add a bit of zest to it all. So we started working with different designers, and two of them were Foale and Tuffin, and then Gerald McCann.

But Foale & Tuffin were unusual because they were tiny and wore mad things like bright yellow and green tights and had this mad sense of humour. Sally's boyfriend was James Wedge at the time and Marion's was Geoff Kirkland. There was always a 'Geoff's Jacket' in the collection. Martin would give the designers money up front to make sure people had enough money to make the clothes. The turnover at Woollands was so fast and it was just mad, and Sally and Marion were very, very, very important to it all because they were always creative but it sold, it was never outlandish. They never did anything that was in any way vulgar. We would work very closely together. It was a real collaboration; it needed to be. On a Thursday I could try out five styles in one fabric, by Friday morning they would know what the order was going to be and it would be in the store by the following Thursday.

It was a funny time; everybody was dying for new things, new shapes – and Sally and Marion got it absolutely right for the time. It was really just a three or four year period when everything new was happening and it was really quite amateur in many ways.

They always had this wild sense of humour. When they were in Carnaby Street they'd go out and just be outrageous. They'd go down Carnaby Street and they'd dyed something purposely some absolutely amazingly horrendous colour. It was always fun to go into the boutique. There was always lots of giggling and laughing, the two of them together all the time. We were all having such fun. And then, of course, The Beatles would pop in and then the *Ready Steady Go!* crowd would pop in because they had to dress up, and they'd be in on Monday and be on the show on Thursday. And that's what happened. There was masses of dancing and going out. If you see Michael Caine's film *Alfie*, that really was the look of what happened at that time, you had a ball on very little money. You'd go to nightclubs, and I remember when the first bistro opened.

Then Sally and Marion got taken up by Paraphernalia and Paul Young and they started doing things out in America; and again, you didn't have lawyers, you didn't have anything, it was all just done. A lot of us didn't make money out of it at all; we weren't all like Terence Conran. Sally and Marion were always very grounded, but the markup on the clothes was so much less in those days. If you

# Vanessa Denza

bought something for £10 you sold it for £15, so clothes were affordable. Laura Ashley also sold to me and their dresses were about £5, but Sally and Marion's dresses were about £12-15, which was a lot of money when you think what everybody was earning. But nevertheless they always got it right. They were always in touch with the right sort of people but there were so few people involved that everybody knew everybody. I mean there was no PR for the whole of Woollands. Can you believe that?

So the press used to come to me for stories, because you were doing new things all the time. There were very good writers like Barbara Griggs and Ernestine Carter. Veronica Papworth at the *Sunday Express* was great. If you got a dress in there we sold hundreds and hundreds of the style. Meriel McCooey did that fabulous *Sunday Times* colour supplement that started in 1962. They were great friends with Marit Allen, I think Marit had a wonderful influence on them too.

The lace keyhole dress – that was *the* dress. That one was the most popular dress, you couldn't get enough, you could put it in anything and it worked. It was copied everywhere. Then they did a whole black and white story, we did lots of versions of that. They were the first to do a trouser suit, it was a corduroy one – red, very fine pin-cord and then they did those simple jerseys but it was so new then, they always got the proportions right and the little detailing like the buttons. And it always fitted, and there was never any problem with fitting.

Then they latched on to the Liberty prints that they absolutely got spot on, and then Cacharel came afterwards. There was the very famous beautiful printed collection that they did with Bernard Nevill, who had also been at the RCA. They really got the right work out of him; they really worked with those prints.

Later they did that look that was the beginning of the whole quilting and ethnic thing; they would move on seamlessly. There

was the tartan story and the layered look. You would really hardly realise it was the same designers and yet it always seemed to have that same edge.

They were great because they would use something traditional like gingham, yet put it in another context. Their designs always had that twist to them. And they weren't frightened of colour. Sally and Marion were great with colour. Manufacturers would offer you the same colours that they had sold for the past fifty years; the idea of trying to move things on was completely alien to most people. It was as if the world had stopped, but Sally and Marion were really, really important – key, key, key – and it was really sad when it stopped.

It was an unusual period, when everything came together. We all knew each other and we were all on the same wavelength. I set them up designing for the Sindy doll. I was approached when I was still head of Woollands in 1962 to design and launch the Sindy doll. I explained to the advertising company, Gray, that I was not a designer but that I would direct the designs and would use Sally and Marion. We launched in the autumn of 1963. They asked me to put on a Sindy fashion show and we had models that all looked young and we had the clothes made up to scale. We compèred the show. I had just come back from holiday, nice and brown, and I remember everyone thought I was a professional compère and stylist.

Sally and Marion's contribution was really extraordinary, but Derek Bibby of Pedigree Dolls, who owned Sindy, would not listen to me when I told him that the fashion styles should not be kept on the shelves for more than a year. This obviously did not relate to the 'action' clothes, just the fashion-based ones. It was such fun, but then Sally and Marion decided they didn't want to do it.

Then they got Barbara Hulanicki to design and launch 'Sindy's little sister' [Patch], but were horrified when all Barbara did was to draw a few sketches. They then pho ed me

back to ask for our involvement again, but I fear it was all a little bit too late.

None of us was paid much but we enjoyed it. People were so much more relaxed about things then, and it was never difficult to work with Sally and Marion.

They had that lovely sense of humour. I don't know if they ever had big money worries or not, but they never let on. But back then big companies like Woollands were much more keen to help and support people, and the RCA played a big part in all that. Sally and Marion always had that get-up-and-go, and the charm, and they were funny. The difference now is that you couldn't be like that; the big companies wouldn't take you on, they wouldn't let you do that. They were all fantastic, incredibly good people but it needed that cooperation and trust. The great thing about Martin Moss is that he let you get on with the job and he let you make mistakes. If Sally and Marion had their label now they'd be told to do the same things all the time, which they never did.

We bent over backwards to work with people. It was a period of real nurturing, but then the second half of the sixties was when the 'big boys' came in and the whole thing completely altered. But in this business you need those very creative shops. In the end the Debenhams board decided Woollands was the thorn in their side, because we were pushing the boundaries the whole time and the board absolutely hated us. They just could not get their heads around this 'awful crowd of people', so they decided they'd sell Woollands. The team was made up of a load of characters that went on to head up interesting new ventures. Terence took a number of people to start up Habitat. Woollands closed in 1966, around the same time that Selfridges launched Miss Selfridge and Harrods launched Way-In. That creative period was about five years maximum, but it really kick-started everything.

Vanessa Denza, c.1963.

**Opposite page:**
Sindy doll, original box
and dress patterns, 1963.
*Photo: Magnus Dennis.*

**Sindy**
the doll
you love to dress

Contact sheet featuring
Sally (top), Marion (bottom),
1963, *Peter Tebbit*.

**Opposite page:**
Jane Asher models navy
and white Liberty print dress,
1964, *David Bailey/Vogue © The
Condé Nast Publications Ltd.*

& Tuffin. My favourite outfit was a black and white check suit. A dress I loved but did not own was an ecru lace one, worn by Peter Blake's first wife when they got married.

I first met Sally and Marion at the Royal College of Art in 1959. They were in the year above me. Then I, with some other students, helped them to make one of their first orders for Vanessa Denza at the Woollands 21 shop in 1963. Following that I stayed on working for them making samples for the factory and grading patterns.

They belonged to a group of women designers that included Mary Quant, but the real queen was Emmanuelle Khanh and the bible was French *Elle*. It was an exciting time, and we really did heave off our bras, and the bust dart disappeared. Heaven came when tights were available, as we all wore our miniskirts with stockings and suspenders until then.

The studio at Marlborough Court had a constant stream of visitors popping in: Cathy McGowan, Keith Moon, Tom Stoppard, Pattie Boyd, Marit Allen. Even Bob Dylan did a photo shoot from the first floor window. There was a lot of partying (for them), especially at the Ad Lib Club, and Friday nights at the Royal College, but there was no partying for me as I had a baby and a toddler. Marion and Sally would get tickets for the TV programme *Ready Steady Go!* I went when The Beatles were on and I got John Lennon's autograph, which I gave to the babysitter.

I thoroughly enjoyed working for Marion and Sally. They were kind and thoughtful, and an inspiration to everyone around them, and we are still friends today. I left because my eldest son started school and I wanted to spend the summer holidays at home. I got a part-time job teaching at what was then the Nottingham College of Art.

# Pauline Smith

Mod illustration, 1966.

Design for Foale and Tuffin Ltd
business card by David Cripps.

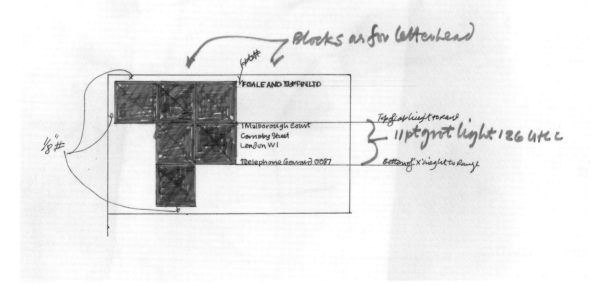

Black wool tunic dress
embroidered with gold Maltese
cross (far left) and brown, beige
and fudge tweed dress with
pompom scarf (far right). *Queen*
magazine, September 1963,
*Maurice Pascal/The National
Magazine Company Ltd.*

**I didn't want to work in fashion.** I just wanted a job. I just wanted to survive. I was living just off the Kings Road and there was coffee culture just beginning. But when I was first working on *Queen* magazine, the convention still was rooted in the fifties. It was still very much London couture as well as Paris, you know. New York didn't figure. The first sessions that I went on were all ball gowns with above the elbow length gloves. It was against those things that I finally found my own voice in fashion and it was supporting the revolution that was the excitement for me. It was with the advent of the 'Youthquake', of the youth movement that I was able to say, 'Well, that was the old order, this is the new order.' You know, in the fifties we didn't wear satin in the daytime, but now that's what we're going to do.

I went in to *Queen* magazine, which was on Fetter Lane in the heart of newspaper land, just around the corner from the *Daily Mirror*, and was led up to the boardroom and to my great surprise Jocelyn Stevens himself came up, who was the publisher of the magazine. And he looked like a young god. He was in his late twenties, early thirties, he had a mane of blond hair and piercing blue eyes. He was wearing a white shirt with coloured braces and his sleeves rolled up, just like a newspaper man. And he talked to me for about two hours and he told me about journalism, he told me about Condé Nast [publishers] and what devils they were and he was there to change the world and he was going to change the world of publishing, and independent publishing was the way to go. So, I was shown a desk in the fashion room and that's how I started.

Beatrix Miller was the editor. Mark Boxer was the art director and in the art department there was a mob of young, unconventional graphic designers who became my friends – they were the ones I made the connection with, not actually the women in my department. I hung out with the people from the art department and we eventually became collaborators and we would do things after hours in our own time and that's how I learned to put together sessions and work with photographers.

Barney Wan was one of the graphic designers, who became my lifelong friend. We had a lot of new young photographers coming in from New York, David Montgomery was one of them, and there was a tiny studio in the basement and we used to work at night and at weekends and I would work in conjunction with the art department. They would say to me, 'We'd love to do some pictures, experimental work with David, can you gather some things together for us.' And we would make photographs and they'd be shown later to the art director and to Beatrix Miller. That led to Beatrix asking me to take on these pages called About Twenty, which was the very, very beginning of young London fashion. She put me together with Caterine Milinaire, who was the daughter of the Duchess of Bedford. And Caterine had a pink mews house in Cadogan Mews and a Mini Minor and I had a cold water flat with a bus. She wore pearls and cashmere and I wore anything that I could find that was funky.

We were working together with people like Foale and Tuffin, Jean Muir, Gina Fratini, John Bates, Gerald McCann – they were all friends, we used to hang out together and go to their workshops and sit around for hours and see what they were up to. It was a sort of time of mutual stimulation and everybody was feeding into everybody else's programme. James Wedge was making amazing hats, Bailey was taking pictures, Jean Shrimpton became a very close friend. You got to know pretty quickly who was interesting.

It wasn't a question of learning or academia, it was a question of this moves me or this feels right, this has the right sort of edge to it, this is something that I haven't experienced before or that I haven't seen before and it was really a question of breaking down the barriers of the status quo, of society. I mean if somebody had asked me to Ascot I would have laughed, I wouldn't have wanted to go. I would have wanted to be seen in the art galleries or the nightclubs or the little cafés.

There was such a strong connection between us all, because we were all excited about the same things. James Wedge was excited about the shape of hats and doing things that had never been done before and Foale and Tuffin were excited about the whole liberation of the female form and the fun that could be had suddenly. Mary Quant had this amazing business set-up when she had Ginger Group and they were fun. You know, Archie, who was the business person, was always behind the scenes, but Alexander Plunkett-Green was witty and entertaining and was incredibly clever with his whole presentation of Mary Quant. And his naming of the clothes as they came out on the catwalk when they did a show would make you laugh out loud. I mean he was really fun and part of it and Jean Muir was very retiring, but very sweet and Ossie Clark was in his own world already, but he was very gregarious at the time. It was just a great fun mix of people and things.

And then there was the Royal College of Art. Janey Ironside, who was the Dean of the fashion school, was a real force to be reckoned with. She was brilliant and she

# Marit Allen

really pushed those people to the degree that they were absolutely ripe to explode at that particular moment and of course there was David Hockney and he was a great friend of all those people. And Derek Boshier and others. There was lots of cross-pollination between those departments as well. It just sort of popped out of the ether at that particular moment in time. I was sorry that I hadn't gone to the Royal College, but there was no time for that, so I was just happy to meet them and they all introduced me to each other, and there we were. All of us, out there!

We [Caterine and I] would go to their workshops. They didn't have backers for the most part, they weren't particularly well organised, there were not necessarily fashion shows. We would know when, for instance, Foale and Tuffin had a new collection ready. They were in Ganton Street, which is just off Carnaby Street, so it was easy, we would just pop round and go and see them and look at the clothes on the rail. They would have a girl who was one of their friends put the clothes on and we'd see the clothes and assess what we thought was the spearhead of what was about to happen or what would come or what would be a fun story to put together and we would link all these elements up and then get them together with a photographer and a story would be born.

Mary Quant was the most famous, she was the first to be famous and she retained that position all the way through. The others were young and struggling and poor and fun.

When I started at *Vogue* magazine was when things really started to generate a lot of international hubbub. I must have moved to *Vogue* in 1964/65. There was a woman who was working at *Vogue* called Lady Claire Rendlesham and she was the one who took the first picture with Bailey and Shrimpton

and she went to New York with them. She was brilliant, she was a wonderful fashion editor. She was haughty and impossibly difficult and glamorous and skinny and a real livewire. She was doing these pages at *Vogue* that were very significant and Jocelyn Stevens wanted her to come over to *Queen* magazine to take over the fashion department. Ailsa Garland, who was then the editor of *Vogue*, contacted me and asked me to replace Claire Rendlesham on the *Vogue* magazine pages called 'Young Ideas' and they were the ultimate pages. I mean they were the pages that we were modelled after on *Queen* magazine, so it was incredibly flattering to be asked to take over those pages.

Max Maxell came over [to *Vogue*]; he became the art director, the youngest art director in London. Max and I were a couple at the time. He was just extraordinarily gifted and very charismatic. He brought Barney [Wan] over and then within months Beatrix Miller became the editor and so very suddenly and quite by osmosis, it became the team that we had had at *Queen*. We developed a new rhythm with the same team on a bigger scale under the *Vogue* umbrella. It was something that you could never have predicted but it worked really well.

In the very early days of the 'Swinging Sixties' we were all taken over to New York by a man called Paul Young, and we were taken over in a private jet and Mary Quant and Alexander, John Bates, Foale and Tuffin, Gerald McCann, myself, Vidal and several others were all bundled on to this plane. We were taken to the opening of the shop on Madison Avenue called Paraphernalia and there was a big party given for us, the Kennedys came and it was really fun. We were taken up to Fire Island and we had a wonderful weekend there and threw each

other into the ocean – it was all very exciting to come from London.

Although I had the highest regard for what was happening in Paris at the time, I always felt that 'Swinging London' was our territory and that it really came from here. You can't underestimate the power of music within that; the Beatles and the Stones most particularly had a lot to do with it.

It was very exciting in London at the time and for instance, Caterine dated Terry Stamp and Edina Ronay, who was her best friend dated Michael Caine. So we were all part of the same thing – Ken Russell, Shirley Russell – they were people that we looked up to. My husband, Sandy Lieberson, was involved with film; he was a producer at the time. He produced *Performance*, one of the seminal movies of the '60s. So I became acquainted with the whole world of film and people in film on both sides of the camera.

We used to use a lot of actors in our stories as well and I took photographs of Jane Asher, Sarah Miles, Samantha Eggar and Julie Christie – I would approach them and ask them if they would be part of a session with David Bailey and they would love it, so we all became very acquainted. So I knew Nic Roeg through Sandy and we became friends and he asked me to do the clothes for Julie Christie in *Don't Look Now*. And before that, I had been asked to put together a really sort of super sixties look for Susannah York in a film called *Kaleidoscope* with Warren Beatty and so I asked Foale and Tuffin to design the costumes and I acted as a sort of co-ordinator and worked with the story and the film people and I was there on set and did the fittings and they designed the costumes. That was really fun to do and that was the first sort of real extension for me of storytelling through clothing.

*This quotation is drawn from the transcription of interviews with the late Marit Allen recorded by Alistair O'Neill for 'National Life Stories' an Oral History of British Fashion project in 2005, catalogue number C1046/13 © British Library.*

Marit Allen models black, red
and yellow voile dress, 1965,
*Bailey/Vogue © The Condé Nast
Publications Ltd.*

**Opposite page:**
'Bowling A Maiden Over' – red and
white striped denim suit. Unused
shot from a session for *Queen*
magazine, June 1964, *Duffy/The
National Magazine Company Ltd.*

Norman Parkinson's group portrait, taken
for *Life* Magazine in October 1963: Young
designers clamber on Chelsea Embankment.
First row from left to right: Mary Quant, 29,
and her husband Alexander Plunkett-Green,
moustachioed Kenneth Sweet, 34. Behind
are Jean Muir, 29, of Jane and Jane, Gerald
McCann, 29, Kiki Byrne, 26, and David
Sassoon, 29. Hanging from lamp post Sally
Tuffin, 25, Marion Foale, 24 and milliner James
Wedge.' © *Norman Parkinson Archive.*

**Opposite page:**
Cover of 'Youthquake' brochure, 1965.

# THE YOUNG ILLUSTRATED
# London Times

IT'S SUPER.*

## New Young London Wave hits the states!
## Quant, Tuffin & Foale Rock the U.S.A.!

*super . . . meaning "okay" according to latest young Britain "slingo"

youth QUAKE®

'Youthquake' brochure featuring Mary Quant
(left) and Foale and Tuffin (right), 1965.

# BRITISH
# CRAS
# ENGLISH
## *CREATING A NEW LONDO*

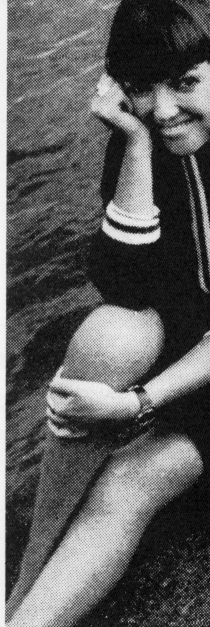

**YOUTHQUAKE ORIGINATOR, MARY QUANT**, is a true Super, meaning Okay designer. For 1965, Mary Quant has designed a completely new breed of fashion for the "way ahead girl who's under 25." First to create the Chelsea Look, Mary Quant is moving away from the "kookie" look with a new kind of clothes she calls "proper but twinklish," "devastating but definitely not dolly." Barnsville, U. S. A. brings this new Quant Look over for the Young Quant·ity market. And gives alert retailers something to hang their increases on . . . and on!

**SEE IT AT BARNSVILLE, U. S. A., 1400 BROADWAY, STARTING JUNE 7.**

# YOUTHQUAKE
## D THE OLD
## ASHION IMAGE
*IR WITH A NEW YOUNG AMERICAN AIR!*

**YOUTHQUAKE COMBO: TUFFIN & FOALE** design for the girl who thinks 30 is old—and wants to look anything but boring. Tuffin & Foale's larky new looks will soar across the country, adding Anglophiles by the millions. Some typical Tuffin & Foale-isms are: colors that clash like cymbals, crazy-mixed-up fabrics, pop arty looks, conspicuous, clever little sleeves, and as they put it "stuff that swings." JP's of Puritan brings Tuffin & Foale to these shores, by way of YouthQuake, 1965!

**YOUTHQUAKE FOR JUNIORS
AT JP'S ONLY
1400 BROADWAY—STARTING JUNE 7.**

**I remember when Alexander and I** went in to do that talk at the RCA we were asked by one particularly obstreperous young man, 'What do you do with all the money?' and we just looked at one another. We didn't know what to say because the business had become so hugely successful so quickly. We hadn't long left art school ourselves – we'd been at Goldsmith's. All the colleges swapped events and went to each other's thrashes.

There were a lot of ideas spilling out in every direction; not just fashion design but music, writers, film and everything. There was so much going on like mad. Art schools really forged a whole new attitude to things. They were very important, brewing all sorts of talent.

At the end of the Kings Road was the Royal Court Theatre, and all the actors and directors like John Osborne and Tony Richardson who worked there brought their girlfriends into the shop. They boosted sales for us. With Bazaar, we were the first of the boutiques and it did cause such a hoo-ha! There were people pouring into the shop but also people complaining. City gents in their bowler hats were really affronted by it, they couldn't believe what we were doing and would bang on the window with their rolled up umbrellas. But soon there were lots of other boutiques, which was great.

Of course I was aware of the Foale and Tuffin boutique and I knew their clothes. They were very, very fresh and very young. Simple, appealing, well designed. Terrific! There was quite a lot of cross-pollination back then, so we'd all meet at the Chelsea Arts Ball and things like that.

The Parkinson photo shoot by the Thames was great fun. There was a real feeling of camaraderie because the fashion industry was quite tough. Instead of being rivals we would tip each other off about a manufacturer, we'd look out for each other.

Our first link with America was when a young man called Paul Young turned up and asked us to design a collection for J. C. Penney. Archie McNair, Alexander and I just didn't believe him. We said, 'Oh, go away, don't be silly!' But then we went over and had a look. The 'Youthquake' trip was quite hellish! Of course, it was terribly exciting doing a city a day, flying chartered aeroplanes with twenty-eight suitcases and a pop group. The Foale and Tuffin girls were on the same trip flying another route. We'd all show up and put on a fashion show with the pop group playing live. There were so many young people who turned up – it was a riotous success. The stores were quite worried because they weren't used to that number of people. That trip really was a killer. It probably lasted about two weeks but it could have been two months! In New York they were actually taking bets whether we would survive that trip. Diana Vreeland showed up at one of the manufacturers', can you imagine, and then she proclaimed in the way she did, "The Brits will see this through!"

# Mary Quant

Clockwise from top left:
Letter from Paul Young at Puritan Fashions Corporation detailing forthcoming schedule, 1965.

Welcome letter from department of public events, New York, 1966.

Sketch for 'Youthquake' collection, Spring 1968.

Sketch for 'Youthquake' collection, Spring 1968.

## PURITAN FASHIONS CORPORATION

*T.W.A. 8 PM*
*730 A M*

*8 PM*

To: Jeanne Kaye     Date: May 4, 1965

From: Paul S. Young

*Reg. 7332*

*# 3   8 174*
*#, 30*

Re: Trip to London

A.  Leave p.m. Wednesday, arrange transportation in conjunction with Sidney Cohn.

B.  Work with Tuffin & Foale at #1 Marlborough Court, London W. 1 (telephone Gerard 0087). The following things have to be accomplished:

    1. Approval of all items to be made that they have not yet seen...these have to be taken to London, together with additional fabric for hats.
    2. Complete color story to be worked out on all items (take sketches of all items with you).
    3. We need at least six (6) additional dresses plus sketches...Bring back all completed dresses plus alternate fabrics and colors plus as many additional sketches as they have. You must have a complete line of additional styles with alternate fabrics and colors and complete approval of everything before you leave London.

C.  Deliver to Tuffin & Foale and to Mary Quant the attached letters, schedule and instructions on English models and itineries etc.

D.  Duration of trip will be p.m. Wednesday, May 5th to Saturday, May 8th.

PSY/sk

cc: Carl Rosen
    Jerry Rosen

---

**DEPARTMENT OF PUBLIC EVENTS**
THE CITY OF NEW YORK
**250 BROADWAY**
NEW YORK, N. Y. 10007
566-4950-51

SHARMAN DOUGLAS
ASSISTANT TO COMMISSIONER

September 30, 1966

Dear Miss Tuffin:

    On behalf of Mayor Lindsay I would like to welcome you to New York and extend our hospitality to you. The City's facilities are at your disposal, and I will be delighted to assist you in any way possible. Please feel free to call on me at the above number.

    My good wishes for a pleasant visit.

    Sincerely,

    Sharman Douglas

    Sharman Douglas

Miss Sally Tuffin
Algonquin Hotel
59 West 44th Street
New York, New York

---

Directors: Marion Foale Sally Tuffin John Stitt

**FOALE AND TUFFIN LTD**

1 Marlborough Court Carnaby Street London W1 telephone Gerrard 0087

*YOUTHQUAKE COLLECTION SPRING 68*
*(3)*

*DRESS Sampled in spot cotton + wool mixture*

*Suggested fabric either stripe or spot fine madras type collar.*

*alternative suggestion. cotton knit from concord interlock 1627 colours. plum olive etc - lime - black with white collar*

*1.*

---

Directors: Marion Foale Sally Tuffin John Stitt

**FOALE AND TUFFIN LTD**

1 Marlborough Court Carnaby Street London W1 telephone Gerrard 0087

*YOUTHQUAKE COLLECTION. (5) SPRING 68.*

*DRESS. - COTTON KNIT. From CONCORD. interlock 1627 colours - sweet pink - sunflower. - Quincquat - bermuda olive.*

'Youthquake' fashions modelled
by Sandy Moss, Pattie and Jenny
Boyd, 1965.

**Opposite page:**
'Youthquake' fashions modelled
by Sandy Moss, 1965

Tuffin and Foale design for Daphne
(division of Puritan Fashions). The news:
**Blazing bands of gold,** opposite page,
round out the top of a blue streak
with short sleeves. About $18. Lace-look
stockings by Le Roi. Bandolinos shoes.
**Funburst,** directly left, radiates from a
low scoop neck to the hipline. Not a
sleeve in sight here! About $18. Stockings
by Beautiful Bryans, Bandolinos shoes.
**Crossword puzzle,** above, spelling out the
streamlined news! About $18. Beautiful
Bryans stockings, Piccolino shoes
**Arrowheads,** right, rocket across a magenta
shift—leaving a trail of orange. About
$18. Le Roi stockings, Sbicca shoes.
All dresses, Alamac bonded jersey of Orlon
and wool. Sketched: wristwatch by
Sheffield, geometric earrings by Freirich.

Daphne dresses, in sizes 3-15J, at Macy's
in New York, R. H. Stearns in Boston,
Dey Bros. in Syracuse, Kaufmann's,
Pittsburgh; Polsky's, Akron; Lazalle's,
Toledo; Rich's, Atlanta; L. S. Ayres,
Indianapolis; De Jong's, Evansville; Bressmer's,
Springfield; Stix, Baer & Fuller,
St. Louis; The May Co., Los Angeles.
For more stores, see page 236.
Accessories stores are on page 238

FLASH!
GEOMETRY!
SUPER!

Famous British team, shown below, composed
Marion Foale, left, and Sally Tuffin. Here
a pooling of views: "Who do we design
for? Ourselves, really...or at least the
girls we'd like to be. We think you Americans
are prettier and more feminine than we are,
but English girls have more of a forward-
thinking look...one that expresses the
moving age they live in. Streamlined is
the word! Our dresses are bright and hard
in their appeal, with a geometric cut.
They're not flowery and soft, and they
should be worn with this in mind.
You need very little jewelry,
or none at all. Perhaps some
geometric earrings, or
a big wrist-
watch.

Shoes with one-inch
should be clean, shiny and
with a geometric cut. Our own models have this look,
and they love it. All for fun. Clothes should show a
heels. Your hair
well-groomed, also
sense of humor, a lively outlook
on life. Quite the opposite of
girls who go out with rollers in
their hair. In England, it's an
arch crime to appear this way!"

TUFFIN AND FOALE

Nenveen.
ypt. 1965.

**As a child I had sewing classes** and I was always making things. My mother and both my grandmothers would discuss everything in terms of what you wore. One of my grandmothers had posh clothes, she went to Molyneux and Victor Stiebel, so part of my 1950s childhood was to be properly dressed – always gloves and a hat.

The one blessing was that I never had to learn to type, I was allowed to draw and sew and go to art school. Although he could ill afford it my father even bought me an apprenticeship for £100 for the year to go and work with Michael Sherard, and there I learned everything that I needed to know about sewing and cutting and where to get things. From there I went to work for Mary Quant. It was about 1960. She epitomised everything that was neat, narrow, girly and amusing. She was very ahead of her time.

In order to pay my way in London I used to sew things at home before I went out to dinner or dancing in the evenings. I had a very pretty, blonde actress friend called Susannah York who had just made a film called *Tunes of Glory*, and I made her something to wear to the premiere. It was the kind of thing I would wear, a velvet off-the-shoulder dress. By 1963 I had grown out of being a dressmaker at night and working for Mary by day and got

a collection together. Kiki Byrne and Mary Quant really were fabulous. They were the forerunners who crept in at the end of the 1950s. They really changed things.

It was in the early 1960s that we all got swept up by America. Macy's department store just arrived and took my whole collection. We were a very small group in London and we all produced young, quite easy-to-sell clothes. Gerald McCann was along with us – he was a very amusing man – and also Tony Armstrong, who was very good at tailoring. Foale and Tuffin's clothes were absolutely delicious, very pretty in a girly way. It was a joyous and innocent time and Foale and Tuffin reflected that brilliantly. They just had that right touch for the time. Sadly I didn't get to wear their clothes, as by then I thought it prudent to wear my own designs.

The Americans were mad keen for us. They couldn't get enough. All the American stores were going mad for the British. They took us to New York and put on crazy English breakfast shows where they served muffins and kippers! Then we were signed with J. C. Penney, which was the biggest mail order business in the States. I got the cover and everything.

We must have all been contacted separately, whether it was Saks Fifth Avenue

or J. C. Penney. I was part of the Macy's venture. It was a gigantic selling operation and we were the product. Somebody must have got us together in New York for a photo shoot for the *Sun* newspaper, and Sally, Marion and I posed together outside the Plaza Hotel in a pony and trap, 'escorted by Ronald Paterson, Edward Rayne and Animals manager, Michael Jeffrey' as the paper said. I was photographed walking down the middle of Fifth Avenue. I used to write a column for the *Sun* briefly until the NUJ questioned whether I had a union card.

In the sixties and seventies there were lots of organisations, people like Cyril Kern, that would help fashion designers to put on shows, and there were lots of handouts for promoting groups of us around the world. I remember on one American trip we travelled to thirty-six cities with a pop group and models, and I can't tell you how much weight I lost. It was like one long party, you would go on stage with the models and there would be go-go dancers and the audience would get up and dance to 'Let's Twist Again' or something like that. It was incredibly good fun.

I did visit the Foale and Tuffin shop and we knew each other to say hello at parties but not to have supper together. There was a lot of 'cross wiring' at the time, especially from

# Caroline Charles

people in the film business, people like Cubby Broccoli, and we all knew John Cowan, Bailey and Donovan. I even got to know Avedon a bit during my time in the America. And there were loads of pop stars – Marianne Faithfull, Lulu and Cilla Black, and actors like Corin Redgrave and Vanessa and Edina Ronay. Foale and Tuffin were part of the same circle. It was a real crossover of photography, theatre, fashion, art and, most importantly, pop music.

I think we were completely innocent of quite how lucky we were. We were all about twenty-one or -two and just thought pages in *Vogue* were all part of the party. Obviously later on you had to concentrate a bit more – after the mid-sixties you had to be nice to someone from *Vogue*, but at that time the American and British press were just interested in the young.

It was a tremendously optimistic time, and when the downturn came in the 1970s most people weren't really involved in politics so they didn't question why the lights went out or that there were strikes at the docks. People weren't really bothered by the nitty-gritty. Those of us who'd been 'dolly girls' had to grow up. We had to make the petty cash balance, and by then we were exporting to the States and selling to twenty-four shops

around the UK. It became a serious business. Nobody taught us about money in art school, so if your bookkeeper was corrupt it all fell apart. Who knew about a costing sheet?

We all sort of made this same little girl dress. In winter it was in flannel, and then you'd make it in lace or add a little collar. It was a very innocent look. The girls always had big hair, dark eyes and pale lips. And then there were the shoes; Moya Bowler had the best shoes. It was absolutely 'Lolita', sexy in a nasty childlike kind of way, and nobody was supposed to speak. It did appear very useful though, as men used to fall for it, but underneath we were very determined young women and full of total grit. Before then our mothers had influenced everything we wore, and that would have been a shirtwaister or dance dress or a proper tweed coat. It felt completely wonderful to be free of that, like we were being allowed out. It was quite different in London, we'd sell in Paris and Milan and they found us very shocking. We were in the streets in hot pants and green boots, doing shows, smoking and just larking about. We were a very tiny group in London who thought we were it, and we were.

Ankle-length white cotton piqué
keyhole dress with organdie turban
by James Wedge, *Queen* magazine,
April 1963, *David Montgomery/The
National Magazine Company Ltd.*

**Opposite page:**
21 Shop advertising featuring
Celia Hammond (left) and Jean
Shrimpton (right) modelling
lace designs, 1963.

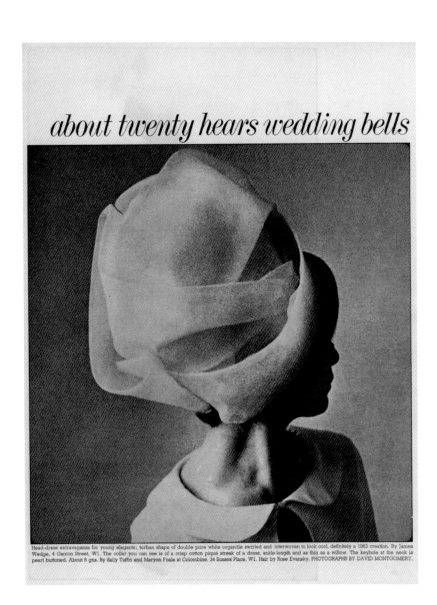

*about twenty hears wedding bells*

Head-dress extravaganza for young elegants; turban shape of double pure white organdie swirled and interwoven to look cool, definitely a 1963 creation. By James Wedge, 4 Ganton Street, W1. The collar you can see is of a crisp cotton piqué streak of a dress, ankle-length and as thin as a willow. The keyhole at the neck is pearl buttoned. About 6 gns. By Sally Tuffin and Maryon Foale at Colombine, 34 Sussex Place, W1. Hair by Rose Evansky. PHOTOGRAPHS BY DAVID MONTGOMERY.

# 21
## shop

By those bright young
trend setters Foale and Tuffin
— a clever use of bedspread
lace to express youth's own
particular brand of formality
The suit in beige
or black 16½ gns
over a crepe blouse in white,
beige pink or black 5½ gns
The dress, crepe skirted,
in beige/black, black/black
or beige/beige £11 15 0
All in sizes 8 to 14
W O O L L A N D S
Knightsbridge · S W 1
M A R S H A L L
A N D S N E L G R O V E
Oxford Street · W1
and BIRMINGHAM

**I remember modelling that Foale and Tuffin** corduroy suit in the Elephant House at London Zoo, but I wasn't sure if the photographer was John French because I didn't have any white gloves on. He was an absolute darling. We did end up in rather odd places. I remember going to Victoria Park in Hackney and he wanted to do a picture by the lake and there were these quite rough lads around and he would say, 'Excuse me, do you boys mind just moving a bit over there,' and they would shout back, 'OK, keep your hair on John', and he thought they knew his name, knew who he was.

Mostly it was exotic locations. The travelling was exciting but a lot of the time you just ended up in a Hilton hotel. We did go to some wonderful places though and got to meet some wonderful people. In Mexico we met with Luis Barragan, the avant-garde architect who painted his buildings these extraordinary colours. You do realise much later how much you took from those people and places, like Avedon, like Japan.

Foale and Tuffin were just starting out when I first modelled their designs. It was the very early days of Woollands. There was Mary Quant at Bazaar and Kiki Byrne, who I loved. Woollands was very unusual. I did the Woollands fashion show, which was quite difficult when you've got no rhythm. Celia [Hammond] was marvellous, she was such a nice girl and she looked so sexy. I think they were a bit worried about her being too sexy. I remember outlining my lips in brown pencil. There were lots of people out of it, but Bailey wanted to keep me naive. In a way I suppose I was too naive to know what was going on.

When you're young you don't really make much of anything. I was in a dream for about ten years and everybody had ambitions for me so I just went along with it. I didn't take much notice of anything really. I just went along with it.

I was one of those girls who was always getting picked up, sometimes it was by dirty old men and sometimes by nice ones. I did a typing course at Marble Arch. I was quite bright at school but I was rubbish at typing because my fingers just wouldn't work. So we would go for our lunch break to the Lyons Corner House [Maison Lyons] at Hyde Park. One day this man shouted over the fence and it was Cy Endfield, who was a director, and he wanted me to do a screen test, but I was appalling on film so he said, 'I think you should try modelling.' So I went to Lucie Clayton [Modelling Agency] and then they sent you to *Vogue*, and soon photographers like Norman Eales and Bailey started using me. Not everybody did. Lady Rendlesham didn't want to use me because I wasn't chic. I was a mess really. But Bailey did. So we did that *Vogue* 'Young Ideas' shoot in New York even though Lady Rendlesham wanted to use a French model called Sophie who was very pretty but more bourgeois I guess.

To go through customs Bailey dressed me in black leather – a trench coat, pinafore dress and thigh-high boots – and he looked like a Beatle, and of course I had my dog's worm tablets on me so it caused a lot of bother. I remember we stayed in this grand place and we were in the maids' quarters right at the top of the building and Salvador Dali was there, and he thought we were quite interesting so Bailey got to take his photograph. I think that session for 'Young Ideas' ['Young Idea Goes West', April 1962] was quite seminal really and started it all off. After that we were more accepted.

Foale and Tuffin were these two very young shy little people. We were coming from the same thing. It was them and Mary Quant who made clothes for young people. We were all in it together. And James Wedge did the hats. It was a young group of people. Bailey was on the same wavelength, he liked a different look and he was very attractive so he could put his hand up the best people's skirts and get away with it! Lady Rendlesham liked him, so that's how I got to go on the New York trip.

All young people party and we did go to clubs. I remember the Ad Lib, but I don't dance very well so I used to take my knitting. And we worked really hard, so you didn't party that much. The sixties were just so different from the fifties; the colours, the drugs, the freedom. For young women it was an exciting time. The pill made you much more free. If you think about how it was in the fifties. *Look Back In Anger*, John Osborne. There was the drug thing, and there were a lot of people who were out of it, but if you worked you couldn't really do all of that. And we weren't a mercenary generation; it wasn't like today. We were never subjected to consumerism in that way. I guess the basis of the optimism was a certain naivety. I guess it was coming after the war, after the 1940s and 50s, that cloud began to drift and there was just more energy, more of everything.

I'm sure I did go to the Foale and Tuffin boutique. Those were the names you remember. Foale and Tuffin's clothes were very pretty, but I'm lazy so I didn't bother with fashion. I would just put on a skirt and an old jumper. I quite like fashion on other people. I was a farm girl; I wasn't really interested in it. I was interested in an abstract way but I didn't want to put it on me. And anyway you didn't really dress up. It wasn't a polished look, it was all about girls like Juliette Gréco and Brigitte Bardot, so I had messy hair and wore any old thing.

# Jean Shrimpton

Opposite page:
Jean Shrimpton modelling a suit
in the Elephant House at Regents
Park Zoo, 1964, *Sunday Times/
Fashion Museum, Bath*.

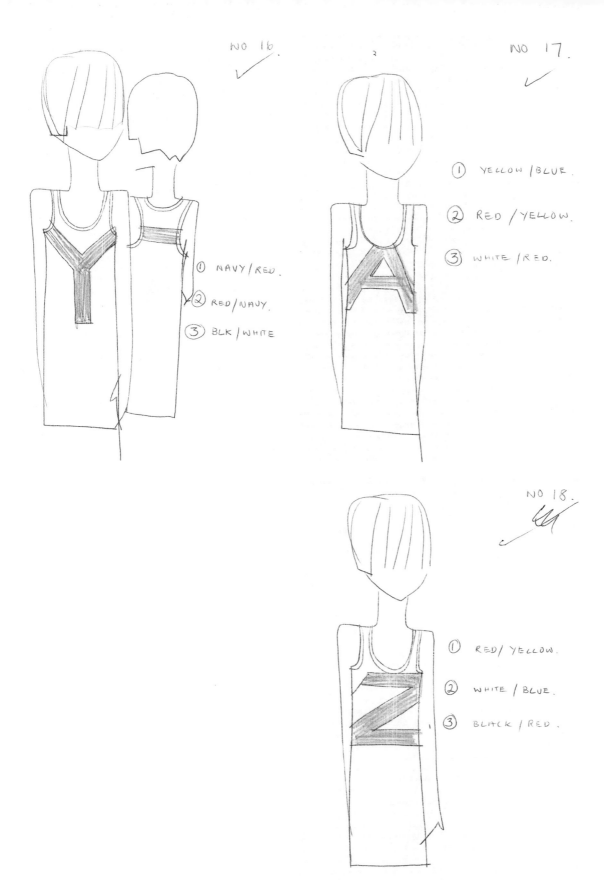

NO 16.

① NAVY / RED.

② RED / NAVY.

③ BLK / WHITE

NO 17.

① YELLOW / BLUE.

② RED / YELLOW.

③ WHITE / RED.

NO 18.

① RED / YELLOW.

② WHITE / BLUE.

③ BLACK / RED.

Sketches of 'letter' vest dresses,
Summer 1964.

**When I arrived in London** it was the last great breath of 'Swinging London', but I loved Foale and Tuffin like crazy. Everyone was copying them, especially in Paris. Before I even came to London I knew who they were and I was hooked into them, mainly because of Françoise Hardy. She was such a huge star, she looked amazing and she wore their clothes. Can you imagine when I was a teenager in Geneva, I was following what they did in *Salut les copains*, the pop magazine for the *génération yé-yé*. For me, Foale and Tuffin represented the revolution that was happening in London. They were all about all that was new. They were before Ossie Clark, before everyone. Mary Quant had her shop but Foale and Tuffin were right there too. They did such fabulous things.

I adored the three-colour dresses that they did. Those bold blocks of colour. I remember them so well. They were fabulous. And I really loved those dresses they did with the big letters. They were absolute genius, just wonderful. And everybody was wearing their clothes in the films; all the famous actresses were wearing their clothes on and off the screen.

It was such a wonderful time, it was so innocent and everything was as fresh as a lettuce. And more importantly, everything was new to me. It was all so new and exciting. It was short, it was snappy, it was new. That period was so incredible. It was because of Foale and Tuffin and what they were doing that I was really discovering what I wanted to do. It inspired me to want to work in fashion. Those women, they made me dream.

Those Foale and Tuffin girls were the discovery of Miss Ironside. All those girls were, all through that period. Nobody really recognises what a genius she was. She was incredible. She was so important. I really want to say that. Thank you Miss Ironside. Can you believe she came to my shop once with Molly Parkin? Can you imagine? I owe Molly so much too. She was the first to use my shoes. She put my first shoe 'The Brick' in a magazine. I loved all those women and I am so grateful to them. Grace Coddington. Diana Vreeland. Molly Parkin. They started my career.

It was such a fabulous time when I came to London. And Carnaby Street; I adored it. I was such a freak! Of course I went to their shop. Are you kidding me? It was such a wonderful place; so exciting, so crazy. I came to live in London because of Foale and Tuffin and what they were doing. I was following all that was going on in England. I would read *Town* magazine and later on *Nova*. How fabulous was Caroline Baker? Foale and Tuffin were really pioneers, along with Mary Quant. And then Barbara came along later. But I really adored Foale and Tuffin the most.

# Manolo Blahnik

**It was an exciting moment of change**, and Martin Moss, MD of Woollands, really was the retail revolutionary of that time. Martin certainly showed a new way forward and it was so exciting to see somewhere like Woollands succeeding in the way that they did, while all the other department stores still felt like these giant mausoleums. I do think Martin Moss very much led the way, and he certainly helped shape a new young aesthetic in this country. He was very important.

I was first shown Foale and Tuffin's clothes by Vanessa Denza, the energetic supremo of the 21 Shop. I was doing the job at Woollands, designing the interior of the new ground floor shop, and Martin rather delegated this to Vanessa. I remember one of the things she did was to put out rails and rails of the kind of clothes she was choosing for the shop. I did the shop with a group of students that I was teaching at the RCA at the time. I did the designing and managed the team and they did a lot of the work, the drawing and that kind of thing.

The interior was very architectural and it was probably the very first minimalist looking shop in the UK. We used pine, big slabs of pine as uprights that went around the whole interior, and then the hanging dress rails ran between these modular uprights. I suppose the look did reflect what I went on to do with Habitat, but the big difference was the scale: the Woollands space was very big and had that big ceiling height. I remember we built a central platform in it, so there was a walkway all around the periphery, and then this central platform that they could use for model displays.

Foale and Tuffin's designs were affordable and that was certainly my philosophy for Habitat, to make things that were well designed and affordable. It was very much the spirit of the time. I would like to call it intelligent design. You can soon spot something that isn't intelligent. They seemed to share that same Bauhaus ethic of wanting to make things that were intelligent, and making design available to the mass market. All of the established designers such as Norman Hartnell and Hardy Amies, they were posh chaps who weren't really interested in the mass market when they could sell very expensive clothes. Suddenly a new breed of designers weren't trying to ape the French couturiers. Instead they were keen to be part of a new modern Britain. The landscape really was changing. It was certainly what it felt like.

I remember thinking that their designs were very graphic, that they were creating the kind of clothes that might have been produced by Bauhaus. It was about trying to be modern. I admired their technical ability and modern style. They were much more fundamental and sensible than the wild pop fashion that was whizzing around at that time. But I also liked their wit. Like their Y-front dresses. What a sensible bit of wittiness!

What I mainly remember about their designs is this idea of simplicity and utility. And good colour. They were very good with their choice of colour.

It was a rather important moment in time. It was exciting for designers to suddenly find they were able to sell things in quantity. It had been a small fashion market up to that moment in time. Then the boutiques in the Kings Road like Quorum and Mary Quant demonstrated what could be done. It was revolutionary. For the first time young people had money and could make their own choice and wanted their own look.

The interesting thing was that designers were just getting enough confidence to do what they wanted to do after being frustrated for so long, taking their clothes around to the various buyers of the big stores and getting the cold shoulder. They suddenly thought, 'Sod it! We'll open our own shops.' Mary definitely demonstrated that it could work, as did Foale and Tuffin and Quorum. And

# Terence Conran

people liked the fact that they were actually getting to meet a designer. It was exciting that the actual creators worked *in situ*. It made it accessible, from weaver to wearer.

I did like their boutique. Again, I liked its simplicity and modesty. I found their attitude and work very similar to my ideas at that time. I felt that it fitted in very well with my own aesthetic.

I think it all changed when the rest of the schmutter trade realised that they were falling behind, and then you got people like Miss Selfridge and Stephen Marks and so forth, doing the job they should have been doing originally. Of course many of the designer shops declined, probably when the designers realised that they weren't such hot business people as they thought they were – when they discovered that the money that went into the tills was not all theirs and that employing staff and so forth, was a complex business. It wasn't all sweetness and light. It's a bit like restaurants, when someone says to his wife, 'you cook so well darling, let's open a restaurant.'

People used to look blank when they asked what I did. A designer? What do you mean? We were industrial artists. We used to be called the Society of Industrial Artists. People didn't really know what designers

did. The biggest change was that it did feel that a large chunk of the public were now interested in what you were doing, and that was helped enormously by the magazines and newspaper colour supplements.

I thought Foale and Tuffin were quite modest for the fashion world, and I liked that. Remember I had been working with Mary Quant and Alexander Plunkett-Green, who were anything but modest. I liked Sally and Marion's demure quality. And they were very young looking.

I'm not really a social person, but there was obviously a certain amount of socialising in the fashion world. It was the era of model girls, high-profile appearance, and people like designers were starting to become celebrities. Also the music scene was a huge influence. That was hugely important. I remember once some of The Beatles came into Habitat to buy some things, and within moments there was this panting crowd at the windows, and in the end we had to call the police.

Sally (left) and Marion (right)
model their Y-front dresses, 1964.

I **first met Foale and Tuffin on the Portobello Road**. My ex-husband, John Jesse, and I had a stall selling art nouveau before anybody really knew what it was, and Sally and Marion were part of a group of designers that would come down every week.

I didn't really buy clothes much before I met them. I used to make my own clothes or pick up things from junk shops. They were really the first people I knew who were designers, who actually designed clothes.

That whole time was fun and the market was wide open. Although we were all seriously doing things, making careers for ourselves, we just weren't serious at all. It was all such fun. We went around in a group and we met up a lot.

I went to art college when I was sixteen to study sculpture. I was carving wood and stone but when I left college I didn't do anything. I got married to John and had a baby. Then I just thought there were no bags around to go with the new clothes that people were wearing. The bags that were around were hard and old-fashioned with snap clasps. I wanted to make things that went with the new clothes so I designed a range of bags with the Sally Jess label. I guess the handles made of Perspex were a continuation of my

sculptures. I was very keen on clean shapes. I worked in Perspex, PVC, plastic, wool and leather. I had a few shapes and I made them in masses of fabrics. I would make them especially to go with people's designs, so I did some in printed PVC to go with somebody's raincoats. The bags tied in with what designers were doing; they were very adaptable. I don't think I made an awful lot to go specifically with Sally and Marion's designs; my bags just sort of worked with their clothes. At that time things just evolved from day to day.

As well as Sally and Marion, I sold my bags to Liberty, James Wedge at Countdown and Bloomingdale's. I sold all over the world because everyone wanted to buy British things.

So I was designing my own label when Sally and Marion asked me to run the shop in Marlborough Court that they had just opened. I got quite involved in things, running the shop, helping choose fabrics. It was all about bouncing ideas off one another. There were always lots of ideas.

John and I went on that wonderful trip to New York for the opening of Paraphernalia that was organised by Paul Young. It was tremendously exciting. We were met by a car

at the airport and taken straight to the Empire State Building and then on to Bob Dylan's twenty-first birthday party. They went mad for us. The Americans hadn't seen anything like us before. There was huge interest because Vidal Sassoon had just opened up his salon next door to Paraphernalia. They were shocked and horrified by the girls in miniskirts. Jenny [Boyd] was there too, modelling. She was married to my brother Mick [Fleetwood] who even did some modelling himself as well before he became a musician. It was just like that.

Working with Foale and Tuffin was very, very wonderful. It was like another family, and I'd wear their things all the time. I wouldn't have dreamt of wearing anyone else's clothes. We were all very loyal like that. There was a family feel.

There was a tremendous feeling at the time for painters, artists, musicians and designers working together. A designer would ask a painter to do fabric for them. I had people paint my handbags. It was very integrated, with everyone working at the same pace.

Sally and Marion called their collections and their designs lovely things like 'Muddy Waters', which was a music reference. I remember when the World Cup was on,

# Sally Fleetwood

they gave their clothes footballers' names. They were very 'of the moment'.

I loved wearing their clothes. I had a wonderful paisley kaftan that I have just given to my tall and slim daughter and I've still got those Double D dresses that Jenny modelled. I've got another called 'Chrysler' after the Chrysler Building that I think was too expensive to make. I wore all their clothes. I loved wearing their trouser suits. I remember when I first went to London my mother said, 'whatever you do, don't wear a trouser suit!' So it was very liberating. Sally and Marion's clothes felt liberating; they freed you up. And they were really comfy clothes; they didn't have those restricting set-in sleeves.

John used to design shirts called FUNSHIRT, made by a proper shirt-maker and I made matching ties to go with them out of the same fabric. I remember John went to the Dorchester and the maître d' tried to turn him away for not wearing a tie. John just flipped up his matching tie and said, 'but I am wearing one!' It was all very naughty like that. I suppose we were just seeing how far we could take things; how far we could push people. It was huge fun. There was a huge furore over somebody wearing their trousers with holes in, even though they were

designed like that. It was on the front page of the newspapers. We were breaking boundaries. It was really exciting. We were a lot of women working together, which was lovely, and I guess we were breaking out, breaking the mould.

And we all travelled a lot and brought things back with us and you'd think, 'how can I use that?' I remember Sally went to Egypt and came back with kaftans but then they'd do them in their way. And Marion was much more a tailor, so they really were a great combination.

That time was just great fun. It was like one big family and we all still know each other. We're all still close.

PVC bag by Sally Jess, 1965.
*Photo: Magnus Dennis.*

**Opposite page:**
PVC bag by Sally Jess, 1965,
with bracelet from Plush Kicker,
1965. *Photo: Magnus Dennis.*

**I left the Royal College of Art in 1964** so I probably did the first collection with Foale and Tuffin that summer. I had been up to Manchester to try and sell my designs to big companies but they were not interested and thought my work was too extreme. I had had an interview with Monsieur Pucci who told me I should do everything in black and white, which is very funny now. Not that I thought that then. Having no success I decided to bypass the classic textile route of selling paper designs and set myself up to produce the actual printed fabric. So I thought I would go and see current designers, so I went to see Sally and Marion and they adored what I did.

I went to see them at their fabulous boutique. They were like the Queens of Carnaby Street at that time. Carnaby Street was so trendy then, with Foale and Tuffin on the corner. There was a whole crowd of us then – Lady Smith, Pauline Denyer as she was, used to do patterns for them.

I had a scholarship to travel but they liked my designs, so I had to spend the time organising the printing of the fabric instead. The prints that were used for that woollen collection were from my final collection at the RCA.

I was one of the first to do prints like that. When I was at the RCA the textiles department was into giant furnishing prints. I was one of the first to go back to doing dress textiles and then I couldn't find a market. Ossie [Clark] used some in his dress show. People didn't do small runs of fabric, but Foale and Tuffin loved it, they loved what I was doing, so then I had to go back to the RCA to find out how to produce what they wanted. That first collection, the lightweight wool, was a real nightmare, because it's really difficult to print pigment on wool. But we did it!

First of all the inspiration was pop art and then they wanted all the black and white abstract stuff – the dominoes and stars.

I think I actually did three collections. The first included a trouser suit with stars on it that was photographed for the cover of *Queen*. The second collection was rows of stars on satin and the third collection was dominoes in black and white. The very last was light bulbs.

There is a great Helmut Newton picture of a crêpe trouser suit. It's a very nice photograph with the girl lying on the bed, and the fan. That print is a bow design. Well, my version of bows.

Then I started teaching two days a week at Ravensbourne and that's how I met Sylvia Ayton and we started doing our own thing together.

Just before I worked with Foale and Tuffin they had done that whole collection using Liberty prints that definitely went on to influence Saint Laurent, although they never get the credit for that.

Their clothes were simple but to the point. I remember having a wonderful purple corduroy trouser suit. I thought I was the bee's knees.

# Zandra
# Rhodes

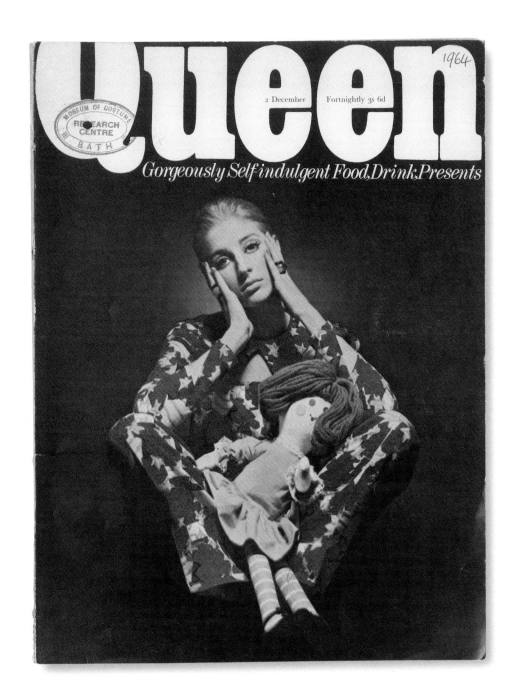

Jill Kennington models trouser suit with star print by Zandra Rhodes, 1964.

**Below left:** Jane Best models star print trouser suit, print designed by Zandra Rhodes, 1964, *Rick Best.*

**Below right:** Shopping in the Kings Road for Foale and Tuffin, 1965.

**Opposite page:** Halter neck crêpe jumpsuit with print by Zandra Rhodes, 1965, *Helmut Newton/Vogue* © *The Condé Nast Publications Ltd.*

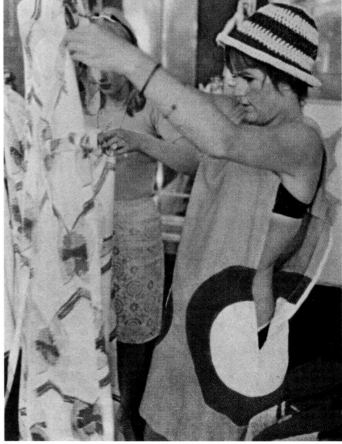

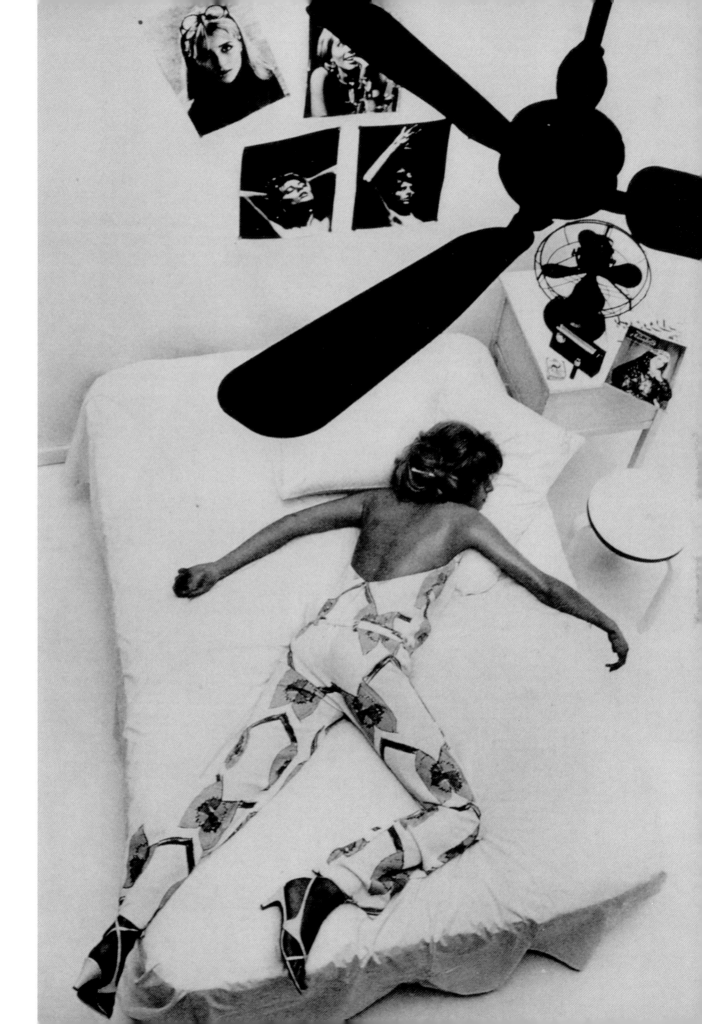

**ANGLOMANIA**

It all began with the Modness that started a few years back in Chelsea. Now the mania for young English fashion is here, there, everywhere. Anglomania's spread to the staidest department stores, but it literally runs rampant in tiny, special boutiques. London has whole blockfuls of them (over there, they call them "bous"), and a new one's just opened in New York. Devoted to fledgling designers both Anglo and American, Paraphernalia's run by Susan Burden (one of June MLLE's Young Smarties), who also models for the shop, assisted by ex-MLLE staffer Betsey Johnson, who also designs for the shop.... This page: Party pajamas, part siren slither, part boop-boop-a-doop, all black-and-white-squiggled crepe. By Foale & Tuffin, about $55. That's Susan Burden, Paraphernalia's model-cum-manager. Her funny, bowed black silk shoes, VanEli. Opposite: Flannel to the floor, the bodice just three buttons deep, the sleeves sheer (i.e., organdy) seduction. By Mary Quant, pale-blue wool, about $70. Pajamas, dress, at Paraphernalia, 795 Madison Avenue. New York 10021

OPPOSITE, PHOTOGRAPHED IN LONDON BY MICH

Opposite page: Black and white party pyjamas sold at Paraphernalia, 1965.

Clockwise from top:
Matching fur beret and scarf by James Wedge, *Queen* magazine, September 1965, *David Montgomery/ The National Magazine Company Ltd.*

Yellow jersey jumper suit featuring matching crochet helmet by James Wedge. *Queen* magazine, September 1965, *David Montgomery/The National Magazine Company Ltd.*

Red and yellow wool crêpe dress 'based on Japanese flag' by James Wedge. *Queen* magazine, September 1965, *David Montgomery/The National Magazine Company Ltd.*

**was at the RCA in the early 1950s.** It was in Ennismore Gardens in a beautiful house and at that time the school was run like a finishing school, with real life debutantes whose mummies had paid for them to go. They all wore princess line coats in Ottoman silk and their voices could cut through steel. Madge Garland, [head of the fashion school] would be in her office. You would go through the front door and another door, and walk straight up the stairs and into her office. The door was never locked. She had an original Marie Laurencin painting on the wall that was worth a lot of money, but her door was never locked. Madge started her life in Bourne and Hollingsworth. She was a shop girl who worked her way up (she became an editor at British *Vogue* and later Lady Ashton) so she wanted the whole place to be rather grand.

It was very genteel and every now and again I would be in disgrace and was sent to Robin Darwin who ran the school. He would just say, 'Have another sherry.' There were only two boys when I was there. Most people were from London but I was from the North of England.

The Foale and Tuffin girls were so sweet. I wanted to cuddle them. We were just this group of young things. We all supported one another. We didn't think about money as being

the most important thing. It was about changing things. We were changing things and that was hugely exciting.

The Foale and Tuffin girls were so adorable but they had this kind of miniature tough attitude, like a Yorkshire terrier or something. You couldn't resist them. The clothes they designed were simple but they said something. I liked their clothes a lot. I loved their stuff. They did nice shapes, kept them simple and always picked interesting fabrics. The girls were not exactly worldly though. They were sweet, a bit other-worldly really, so I felt very protective of them.

Sally Kirkland, the fashion editor of *Life* magazine, was a very powerful lady. She had just made Italian fashion happen and had been given an award by the Italian government. I had met her before in London and had taken her for some very potent dry martinis at a hotel off Berkeley Square. She never forgot that so when she came back to London I was her first port of call. She wanted to know what was happening in 'Swinging London', so she photographed all of us by the Thames. I remember Norman Parkinson was the photographer. He was a really sweet man and we later became friends, him and his wife Wenda. That was a very funny day; he made everyone laugh. It's very funny because in the

# Gerald McCann

What America didn't really get at that time was the discotheque, which was the place where all those girls in London would wear those clothes. It's funny because they all looked identical in their little dresses. The Americans had places like Arthur's, but even when they wore the right clothes their hair was wrong; they were too done up, and they often looked ridiculous in the clothes.

I was the only one of us British designers with a proper manufacturing base so I would get big orders. The biggest seller I had? I had gone to Liberty and all the nannies were buying this fine cotton with a little print on it to make children's clothes. It was so lovely. So I bought some and made this little frock. The girls in the showroom liked it so I called Woollands and went to see Vanessa but she said she didn't have the budget left to buy it so I said, 'Well, I'll send you three dozen and if they don't sell I'll take them back.' I delivered them in the morning and by late afternoon she called and asked if she could have another three hundred!

I remember another dress I did for Peter Robinson, it was called the 'Nō' dress – in white wool with a khaki suede belt and wide sleeves for travelling. Barbara Griggs had photographed it and I got a call from the store

— they had four hundred women in the store looking for the dress they'd seen in the newspaper. They were exciting times. You had to get to the stores and then you had to get to the buyers and push yourself to them. You were constantly repeating your storyline over and over. What it all meant. We were all a bit timid except Vanessa, because she had already got her clientele sorted – she'd got Foale and Tuffin, Jean Muir, and Roger Nelson. I got in there [Woollands 21 Shop] late because I'd been at Fenwick.

Martin Moss, who ran the store, was the sweetest man in the world. He called me into his office and said, 'We keep losing stock – can you help?' I said, 'Do you have cleaners?' and he said, 'Yes', so I said, 'Do they have large wicker baskets?' They discovered a whole gang!

I knew a lot of people. John Stephen was doing fabulous menswear and then there was the wonderful George Malyard, the Welsh milliner. I remember Rita Tushingham wanted a hat so he made a peaked one and put a photograph of her wearing it in his window and sales went wild. It was so much fun because everybody got on so well. You felt as though you were breaking new ground. It was all so innocent.

Foale and Tuffin sketches including
*Kaleidoscope* designs, 'Napoleon' coat
and Double D dress, 1966.

**Opposite page:**
Pattie Boyd models 'Napoleon' coat,
1967, *Richard Dormer/John French*.

Buckles. *Photo: Magnus Dennis.*

**Opposite page:**
Twiggy models cotton corduroy
zip suit, 'at Marit's flat with her cat',
1967, *Helmut Newton/Vogue*
© *The Condé Nast Publications Ltd.*

Opposite page:
Contact sheet featuring Grace
Coddington modelling Varuna wool
Liberty print keyhole dress,1963,
*Vernier/Alexander/Carapetian.*

Sherbet pink sweater dress,
1964, *John Adriaan/Sunday Times/
Fashion Museum, Bath.*

*Ready, Steady, Go!* **was terribly important**, and you have to remember that one lived one's life around that show. We would go down to the TV studio and there would be all these amazing people hanging out there. It was incredibly exciting. When Cathy [McGowan] wore the clothes it meant that everyone would come down to the shop to buy that particular look. So you'd send the clothes out to Cathy in the afternoon of the show and watch that evening on TV to see which ones she had chosen to wear. Would she wear a Biba dress or a Foale and Tuffin? I was green with envy when she chose 'Tuffy Fluffies', as Fitz [husband, Stephen Fitz-Simon] called them. Cathy has worn a "Tuffy Fluffy"!' he would say. We used to hate it. I suppose it's like the Oscars now. At that time we only had one pattern, so it was about varying the fabric. I remember when we got editorial on a purple dress with a lace collar; it was a nightmare because the only purple fabric we could find was a pair of purple curtains.

Sometimes Cathy wore Laura dresses, imported by Top Gear in the Kings Road. Laura was a shop in the suburbs of Paris; the designer there was Sonia Rykiel, who was making these amazing dresses that Brigitte Bardot used to wear. The shop I was most envious of was Top Gear. It was run by James Wedge and Pat Booth. They imported the most beautiful of French clothes, the sort that appeared in French *Elle*. French style was hugely important, but not the fashion shows. It was *Elle* magazine. It was the way in which *Elle* edited everything. The wonderful colours. That was the only magazine. When we did go to Paris we would always rush to one or two specific shops like Laura, but it was only really in England that people were wearing the stuff. In Paris everybody wore something new, but they all wore the same thing.

I was first aware of Foale and Tuffin when they were in Woollands, way before we started doing our thing. I was working as a fashion illustrator and most of the time the clothes I was sent to draw were revolting. My job was to make them look fabulous in the drawing. It was really frustrating because although I was earning money, I couldn't find any clothes that I wanted to spend it on. I was being sent to the Paris shows and I felt like the country cousin. I nearly died when I saw their check suit.

When I went to art school I realised that to be a designer was going to take years, and I thought I would never make it. I really didn't see myself in a workroom picking up pins, which is what you had to do when you started. I went to Brighton Art School and it was run by Joanne Brogden, who went on to be the head at the RCA. She was an amazing teacher and she said that my making up was so dreadful that I had better concentrate on drawing. So when I graduated I applied to a studio that specialised in fashion illustration and I got my first job. I got £5 a week.

At the beginning it was awful because all the senior illustrators got the best jobs and I was making the tea. Later I graduated to drawing corsets. When I met Fitz he told me that I should go freelance. I was terrified, but soon everything started rolling and I got jobs drawing for the magazines in Paris and Italy. I would be sent to the collections. It was incredibly hard to draw and remember everything. You weren't allowed to have the clothes until a month after the shows. A journalist was allowed to see two garments on a model for about five minutes. So if you went to the shows you had to remember everything. When they ended everybody would rush out to the nearest cafes and start sketching. When buyers bought a ticket to the shows for a huge amount of money it entitled them to two toiles that they could take away and remake the outfits for their stores.

Starting up Biba was totally spontaneous. I wanted to be like Harrods or Fortnum & Mason. I was very ambitious but the production was always a nightmare. At the

# Barbara Hulanicki

beginning it was an absolute horror. I was terrified all the time. How will those trousers turn out? What are we doing? Maybe that lack of knowledge was our strength, as it let us do things.

It was really so different then because you could open a shop just like that, whereas now you need huge investments from the banks to open a shop on the High Street. When we opened our first shop I don't think we even signed a lease. We just paid the twenty quid a week. Fitz was really good at finding strange premises. The second one was on Kensington Church Street: he found this great grocer's shop and traced the owner, who turned out to be a phrenologist, and he said, 'OK, your head is a good shape' and then he asked to see me and I passed the test, so that was that.

I never really left the High Street [Kensington]. We opened our first shop there because we lived around there and Fitz came across this wonderful chemist shop in Abingdon Road. A lot of people travelled in those days because the train fares were cheap. They would come to our shop from all over England. Fitz and I never really wanted to be near anyone else.

Carnaby Street really was quite rough, you know. We were quite snobbish about around there. In the Kings Road there was a lot of

promenading but there weren't many boutiques. The person, who was fabulous, even before Foale and Tuffin, was Kiki Byrne. Her shop was on the Kings Road where Jaeger is now. I can remember standing in front of the window and I nearly passed out. 'Oh, what a wonderful little black dress!' It seems so stupid now.

We were all dressing a generation who were newly independent. They didn't have to ask their mother's opinion and they didn't want to wear their mother's clothes. At that time you had the choice of going in two directions: you could go the fifties route, which meant a row of pearls and wearing your hair in a chignon, which made you look like you were thirty! I hated it. Real pearls, Yuck! You would buy two outfits a season and wear them until they dropped off you. I didn't want that. I wanted new things to wear. With Biba, women would come in every week to buy a new dress.

I never did go to the Foale and Tuffin boutique. We all hated each other in those days. I never met anybody. We all holed up in our little workrooms. I know that Ossie Clark hated us. But there were a lot of interesting people around; people who hadn't made their name yet – film-makers and musicians. There were a lot of fabulous people coming from

America at that time. Once you opened your front door, it was amazing who came through it. Also we had very beautiful girls working in the shop. They were like a magnet. I remember one day Marcello Mastroianni came in. He actually looked a bit suburban. He kept asking the girls out on a date but they were like, 'Oh, he's much too old!' In those days young girls didn't go out with old men.

Being part of a duo was crucial. You have to do that job with someone, you really do; preferably with someone not doing the same as you. That's what was so wonderful for me and Fitz. He was amazing because he did all that side of it, the production, and he loved it. It was a boy's dream for him working it all out.

From 1969, for us, was the best time because we really knew what we were doing by then. We had the money to spend and we had our manufacturing set up properly. This had constantly been our worry; we just had to keep going. If you stopped then you fell apart. And there was another generation ready to come up.

Marion at sewing machine,
1963, *Tony Evans*.

**Opposite page:**
Photo session featuring
Marion and Sally, contact sheet,
1964, *Michael Seymour.*

I **was on the 'Observer' in 1964** and then joined the *Sunday Times*. Brigid Keenan was on the newspaper and I was on the magazine. I'd known her since the *Express* days.

I came across Foale and Tuffin while doing the rounds like we used to in those days, tramping the streets and going out to the studios for a story. You might pick up someone new from a fashion show or even from a picture in another publication. You'd think, 'Oh, that looks interesting, I must go and see that.' I used to do the real nitty-gritty business of going to their workroom to see their clothes. I remember sketches pinned up on the wall, and rails of half-made clothes, work in progress. I wasn't part of their entourage but I knew them from just doing the rounds. I knew Marion, but I think I met Sally later through James Wedge.

What Foale and Tuffin were doing was really interesting, absolutely. They were among the young swingers, the new face of fashion. They were really good, and their designs were extremely deft and very amusing. They were exactly the kind of things that we were looking for, and that went down well with young people at the time.

They showed a lot of talent, and talent was a really good commodity at that time. You didn't become a celebrity in those days because you were seen out at nightclubs, you became one because you were doing really good work. Like Ossie and the rest, Foale and Tuffin were celebrated for what they were doing. It was always interesting and fascinating to see what they were doing next.

Everything was going on in London at that time. It was like a big club really, and you had to be talented to become a member. You

had to be producing something amazing; you had to have a credential, a form. Everybody knew everybody, and we all had enormous respect for each other.

Very early on you could tell Foale and Tuffin were extremely talented. What was great was that they were producing on a level that was affordable; when you went shopping you knew you could afford the latest thing. They started trends that you could buy immediately.

Foale and Tuffin's clothes reflected the times – they were very young and girly. All those flowery prints and motifs; when you went into a room it was like a garden of flowers. We'd been stifled in the 1950s. Coming out of the war everything felt so stuffy and heavy. You felt that you were encased in your clothes, they were so inhibiting; even underwear was inhibiting. I remember I would go to photographer John French's studio and even the reed-thin models like Barbara Goalen would be pulling on these elasticated roll-on suspender belts and corselettes.

Foale and Tuffin's models looked perfect from head to toe, with those funny little schoolgirl shoes, and so colourful. Fashion at the time projected a youthful look – the flowers, the lace, even the knee socks and funny little boots. I remember when Courrèges came along and knocked the heels and toes off boots. I went to tell Ernestine Carter about the collection I'd just seen and she said, 'Don't be silly dear, you've been drinking!'

What happened was that everything was moving so quickly, so people were thinking on their feet. Things would be terrifically popular one day and then you'd move on quickly to the next thing. It was an incredibly exciting

time, it was tremendously exhilarating. You were never bored with fashion, you just enjoyed it.

Like much of London at that time, Foale and Tuffin really did swing. What they did attracted a certain crowd. It was the adventurous crowd that caught on really quickly. I remember Terence Conran's Soup Kitchen, and buying all those things in Habitat – the bookcase and the little desk – all the new things that we bought. And publicity was good then, there was a lot of publicity about the new fashions.

I loved their trouser suits. It was very much, 'if the boys can do it so can we'. We were much tougher then. Before then you only saw someone like Marlene Dietrich in a trouser suit and thought how extraordinary she looked. Suddenly they didn't look like boys' clothes any more; they just looked modern.

Foale and Tuffin blossomed with the era. They had so many ideas knocking around. It was delightful. You were never short of something new and fresh to feature on your pages. They were very 'on the button' and they seized the moment. It was a great time to be alive, and be working in that milieu. The fashion industry wasn't as big then and perhaps the biggest difference is that money talks now, whereas nobody seemed to be worried about money then – it didn't seem so important. People were more concerned about the design of something looking good. Looking back, it was really refreshing.

# Meriel McCooey

White cotton drill suit with navy and white Liberty print collar, 1964, *Sunday Times/ Fashion Museum, Bath.*

**It was around 1962**, as I was looking at the work of new and young designers in London to feature in the magazine's fashion pages, that I first became aware of Foale and Tuffin. I was about nineteen years old. I had been working at *Queen* magazine, hired by the editor-in-chief Jocelyn Stevens as a fashion editor, and was teamed with Marit Allen. Together we devised the 'About 20' pages as the new youth-fashion orientated pages, in order to set us apart from the traditional couture fashion that had been featured so far in this venerable old-fashioned society magazine. We did one fashion story with Ivy Nicholson as the photographer-cum-model. I was in the picture wearing a knobbly knitted pull-on hat, peering from under the armpit of film producer David Cammell on a bridge. I had quite forgotten about that shoot! We did another at my stepfather's ancestral home Woburn Abbey.

Marit and I were constantly bouncing from one design studio to another, exploring the designers' possibilities. Foale and Tuffin were hard-working busy bees with not that much time for socializing, but they were friends with the likes of Mary Quant and Barbara Hulanicki.

The Foale and Tuffin girls were such unusual and kind young women that one could not help but like them. Their clothes presented such a departure from the traditional dowdy tweeds, plain cotton and velvet trims associated with the proper, classic outfit worn by British people who cared about their look, yet they used the same materials in a very light and whimsical way. I remember in the summer wearing a loose smock-type dress made from tiny black and white floral print Liberty lawn cotton, with a square neckline made of lace. I wore it for decades; it had a timeless style. I would still be wearing it today if I had not washed it to shreds.

They were not trailblazers. Their style had more to do with designing clothes you could look unusual wearing but be comfortable in; outfits to wear everyday to work, rather than loud flash-in-the-pan designs. Showing off was not Foale and Tuffin's currency. Personally they were shy and hard-working. Their success definitely set the tone for other women who were looking at working in that field. They were totally in tune with their age group. Yet they could bridge the gap between the young women's classic upbringing and their desire for new looks, by using traditional fabrics with easy, loose-fitting shapes and whimsical details, such as their trademark swallowtail pointed collars.

The early and mid-sixties, in retrospect, were very free-form in London. It was a time of innocent exploration. There was enthusiasm for cross-pollination of the various artistic forms. The overall mood was to stretch the genres, and render life in cheerful notes and mixed colours. It was an affordable proposition created at a leisurely pace. London did not feel crowded; there was room for enterprising souls to set up experimental studios and shops in odd locations.

Fresh talents were popping up everywhere; fashion, music, stores, discos, media, restaurants were re-energizing the English landscape. The tweedy traditional style of England was getting a makeover. Energetic youth was reshaping the time. It was as if a grand old lady had been woken up from a long slumber, and her grandchildren were taking her on a wild dance down Oxford Street.

# Caterine Milinaire

White cotton keyhole dress,
*Queen* magazine, July 1963,
*Ivy Nicholson/The National
Magazine Company Ltd.*

**My first impression of Foale and Tuffin?** Sheer magic. What they were doing was utterly different to anything anyone had done before. They were a pair of the most unlikely people to be doing what they were doing. They were so quiet and so 'unflashy'; they were both extremely shy and private people.

I wasn't so much in the Foale and Tuffin coterie, I would have liked to be but it was a bit of a private little group and I was on the outskirts. I would have liked to call myself a friend but I wasn't really. I didn't know them that well personally. I was more a worshipper.

At the time I was a fashion editor at *Vogue*. I was doing mostly underwear, gloves, and weddings. I did fourteen pages of Grace Coddington by Parkinson. It was the Lycra revolution in corsetry, and stockings became tights – they were thick and coloured and had clocks on. I then became a more general fashion editor, and did the 'More Dash Than Cash' pages. I was an extremely close friend of Marit [Allen], but I never did young fashion as such. She was more innovative, I was a reporter. I was an observer, a very good observer. We got on because we were so different.

I'm Australian and had always lived abroad. I came to England at nineteen, and my job and my lifestyle were inseparable. It was one excitement after another; the excitement of living that day. I danced on *Top Of the Pops* and went out with Alan Freeman. Both Marit and I married alternative men. I married a journalist who was features editor of *Vogue*. We were all involved in each other's weddings and things, and it was fashion in everything – fashion in the movies, in opera or films. It felt like a whirlwind of electricity in the air. It fired you. There was so much energy and excitement; you were always seeing things. Remember, most people who were in the 1960s had lived through a bit of the 1950s, and that's important. We lived to the full. I went to some outrageous parties.

I went to the Foale and Tuffin boutique as often as I could. It was only one step away from the office but it was terribly small. I remember Pattie Boyd being in there, and Marit of course. I think their clothes were magic, they made you feel just wonderful. When they had a new collection I was 'wowed'.

My favourite outfit was a purple corduroy trouser suit. It was simply amazing, and I wore it with a yellow sweater underneath. The jacket was double-breasted, cut a bit like a tuxedo. It went below the waist and had flared, I suppose boot-cut, trousers. It may have been Marit's, because she sewed on these wonderful mother-of-pearl buttons from the Button Queen. I remember walking down the street wearing it and I knew I looked wonderful. Wherever you wore any of their clothes, that was the occasion.

Wearing that trouser suit I couldn't have felt more liberated, sexy or free. It transformed you when you wore it. I think it has to be one of my favourite garments of all time.

I also had the dresses in tiers of different prints, which were ravishing, and the first waistcoat I had was in Liberty lawn, with ties. It was purple, with all sorts of flowers. It was divine! I also had a wonderful red felted wool smock, like a shepherd's smock. I can feel it, I can touch it! I could wear that smock today. You always felt like nothing could go wrong when you wore their clothes.

I think they had a profound understanding of the electricity in the undercurrent. They were drawing up things from the air of inspiration. They had it in their fingertips. They were like little elves making magical things.

It is interesting that they split up in the early 1970s, as some of the magic had gone out of it all. I think they were immensely important to British fashion; they practically invented it. And they were terribly English with all the Liberty prints. They were an absolutely integral component.

It was their clothes that I think of most, the longing for their clothes, like I longed for the Mary Quant ruffle shirt in Bazaar. But that was just one shirt; with Foale and Tuffin it was everything they did.

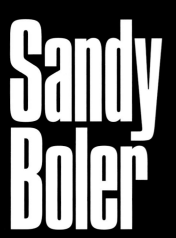

# Sandy Boler

Opposite page:
Corduroy trouser suit,
c.1966. *Frank Cowan.*

Cowboy-style black and russet
corduroy trouser suit and 'the shortest'
Mod miniskirt, 1966, *Traeger/Vogue*
© *The Condé Nast Publications Ltd.*

**first knew about Foale and Tuffin** through my sister Pattie who was already modelling. She had the first dress by them that I ever saw. When I saw it I was like, 'Ooh, I love that dress!' and it was a Foale and Tuffin. She'd got it from Woollands 21 Shop. It cost too much money for me but I was pretty knocked out by it. I thought it was very different and young looking. Then Jane Asher came around the flat where I was staying – it belonged to George [Harrison] and Ringo [Starr] – and I remember she was wearing a Foale and Tuffin dress too. So I was aware of them before I met them.

I was at school in Holland Park starting my sixth form, getting ready to do my A-Levels. I had a scary boyfriend who'd been in a band called The Cheynes with Mick [Fleetwood], who was later to become my husband, but the band collapsed so the boyfriend took up doing a bit of interior decorating. Mick's sister Sally Fleetwood said that Foale and Tuffin had just moved into their new premises and so he went and decorated it. While he was there they told him they were looking for a new model to do house modelling, and he told them they should see his girlfriend. I hadn't thought of leaving school, so it was my first interview for a job anywhere and I was really shy, but they liked me so I started the following week. I just left school, I didn't talk to my parents or anything – but we were a bit of an odd family.

I joined them when they were just about to have the shop, so I was upstairs in their office. They were about to do the collection, so I would go across the road to the studio and Marit Allen and the other top editors of the magazines would come in, and I would wear the dresses and walk up and down. After a while some of the editors asked to use me for photographic shoots, so I would model for their magazines and newspapers wearing Foale and Tuffin clothes.

When the shop had opened and it was quiet and I wasn't needed to model, I would go and work in the shop. That was the wonderful thing about working with Sally and Marion, it was so carefree and I got all the samples available to wear. I had a wonderful red trouser suit that made me feel completely *me*, like I was my own person. Their clothes were all about self-expression. I spent my entire pay packet, all of £5, on a pair of Moya Bowler shoes to go with that trouser suit.

The workroom was off Carnaby Street. You went up a rickety narrow staircase with creaky floorboards. The office was very old-fashioned, a tiny room. At first there was only one secretary and then another girl joined her. There were lots of magazines and papers all over the place. The studio across the road overlooked Carnaby Street. They had made that very modern-looking, there was lots of light and it felt very spacious. There was a big table and lots of patterns and material and a clothes rail full of samples.

The boutique had rails of lovely clothes, but mostly I remember the great music. Again it was not terribly big but I remember big mirrors. What was more of a hang-out was the street itself. The guys from the men's boutiques would walk up the street and pop in for a chat, or I'd walk up the street to the boutiques where they worked and chat to them.

Then there was the whole 'Youthquake' trip. I went with them to America. This was the very first trip. Pattie came too but I stayed longer. I was seventeen years old so it was mind-blowing just being in New York. What really blew me away most was the way in which Paul Young and those other businessmen, these big, important heads of the garment industry, all behaved like big overgrown children. It freaked me out. They treated us like mannequins, not like real

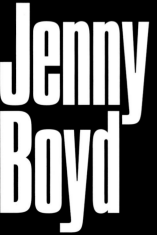

# Jenny Boyd

people. Sally and Marion treated us great. They were more like friends.

I remember during that trip dancing at Arthur's, which was a new club. Vidal had just opened his salon there. It was all new and exciting but most wonderful of all was the music that was played on the radio – fabulous Motown tunes. Music you'd never heard in London. It felt like the world was opening up for you. It was incredibly exciting. It was fast but at that age things are changing all the time. Sally and Marion really coincided with the music and attitude of the time perfectly.

Favourite outfits? I had my red trouser suit but then I had lots more. I had a white trouser suit and then a fabulous corduroy trouser suit. I loved them so much because when I was younger I lived in trews; remember this was before jeans. Gosh, they sound so ghastly. I used to worry that when I grew up I'd have to wear suspender belts and proper dresses and smart suits but now there was none of that. Most of all, the trouser suits symbolized fun; having fun, feeling easy, being who you were. They felt like *your* clothes. I could wear them to do anything. They were so timeless. I would love to have them now. Sally and Marion really complemented each other – Marion made

the trouser suits and Sally was responsible for the pretty dresses. The combination was fantastic. I loved their dresses too. I had a lovely black satin dress. I just loved *all* their dresses.

I think it was like a family. They knew Mick and Mick's sister, so it really felt like one big family. Everyone knew each other, and Sally and Marion were such fun to be with. It was all so light-hearted and fun. I still see them and it still feels exactly the same. I feel very lucky that that's how I started my career, my introduction to having a job. It just didn't feel like a job. I was incredibly lucky. And best of all was that they didn't mind if I came in late a little hungover or a bit stoned. They were just great.

Opposite page:
Pattie Boyd (left) modelling yellow,
lime and white daisy dress and
Jenny Boyd (right) modelling pink
and turquoise rainbow dress,
c.1966, *Sidney Pizan*.

Jenny Boyd modelling Double D
dress, 1966.

Contact sheet featuring
black and white rayon crêpe
'Sprint' dress, 1964.

**Opposite page:**
'Hoot' white suit, Yardley
Look award, 1966.

In 1964 I won a guest editorship at *Mademoiselle* magazine and came to New York. While working at the magazine the editor suggested I should be a fashion designer and told me to go see Paul Young, an English guy who was about to open Paraphernalia (a new shop at Madison and 65th Street). I did some crayon drawings to show him and I got the job. I quit *Mademoiselle* in 1965 and started designing full-time for Paraphernalia.

It was the hip, new, far-out, cool boutique just a few doors down from Vidal Sassoon's new salon. It was a lofty, wide-open space of glass, wood, mirrors and chrome filled with rock'n'roll music and Go-Go dancers in the windows. The logo for the shop was a black and white target. It housed my favourite designers along with a New York stable of young designers who worked with me. It was so new and exciting. It was a great hang-out point for the young, rich and funky, from Warhol superstars to Jackie Onassis. There were a lot of parties. It wasn't about the prices but the look. It sold young fashion. It was really the only place in New York you could get the new 1960s clothing. Truly the first time for art as fashion, fashion as art. Young New York designers lasted as long as the clothes sold. I was one of the very few who lasted, and I still cut and make the same patterns as back then. In 1967 Paraphernalia was franchised and there were shops all over the country.

Paraphernalia sold a European-American mix of designers including Foale and Tuffin, Mary Quant and Emmanuelle Khanh. I loved the Foale and Tuffin girls, personally. They were very funny and crazy. I remember our rock band trips, especially in the store in LA next to The Derby. I only really saw them at appearances but I thought they were the best pantsuit designers I ever knew of, and that they influenced everyone right up to Yves Saint Laurent, but they never got the credit and distribution. They had a very Julie Christie-esque style and they cut the best jackets. They were my favourite along with Mary Quant and Biba. But I mostly wore my work and they wore their work. We were living the Youthquake time zone; in theory, all designing for ourselves, really.

I took my first trip to London when I was a guest editor at *Mademoiselle*. That trip opened me to the London Mod, rockness, and fashion, and made me know that I wanted to make clothes. I never knew that before. It made me realise I wanted a piece of this, that I felt the same way and was on the same page. That trip changed my ideas about life. I loved it, died for it, worked it. I was so inspired. London was the leader in fashion, music and hair-dos at that time so it made sense to have it in America.

We were landing on the moon and throwing our bras away. My clothing had to look modern and clean. Motorcycles and NASA inspired me. During my guest editorship at *Mademoiselle* I assisted the fabric editor for a month and found out all about modern fabrics. It was the time zone of synthetics. I designed striped T-shirt dresses in rayon jersey and tight sexy dresses with lots of zips like a motorcycle jacket. I also did a look based on English schoolgirls and another that was a fringe hippy style. I was influenced by the times, by rock'n'roll and a new generation around Warhol and his Factory people, Timothy Leary, The Velvet Underground, Allen Ginsberg, the Chelsea Hotel and Max's Kansas City, which paralleled The Beatles and The Stones, etc. Edie Sedgwick [New York socialite, Warhol protégée and Johnson's fitting model] was a light, sweet friend with the perfect Twiggy body.

It was the most brilliant, creative, brand new kind of revolution. It was about revolutionary ideas and new geniuses *à la* Bowie, Joplin, Jagger, Hendrix. But it was crazy and everybody was off the wall with energy, mostly synthetically enhanced by diet pills to LSD, you name it.

Everyone was passionate about expressing whatever they wanted to, whether they were dancers, writers, singers, artists or designers. It was a time when everyone collaborated, connected and talked to each other. I don't really know how many of them actually ended up successful. Looking back, it was the best place ever. While in it, I thought of nothing but just doing my work.

My style heroes were all the people who were on this new Youthquake train. And the English people really led then.

# Betsey Johnson

EVENING STANDARD, MONDAY, JANUARY 4, 1965

# WATCH OUT FOR THE
## CLASH: MODS v. ELEGANTS

## griggs predicting '65
## fashion

But the outstanding feature of Fashion 1965, as I see it, is going to be the Great Clash between the Mods and the Elegants. And as a girl with a guaranteed ringside seat throughout, I am filled with joyous anticipation.

On the one hand, the Mods, whose heroes are Courreges, Tuffin & Foale, the 21 Shop, James Wedge, Vidal Sassoon, anyone young and fast with decided, challenging ideas about fashion. Mods like their fashion to be very much on the young side, racy, fast-changing, a bit absurd if necessary, and not necessarily either pretty, flattering or wearable.

On the other hand, the Elegants, few of whom will see 20 or 30 or even 40 again, who feel they've had a raw deal over the last five years; who long for clothes to be expensive, beautiful, elegant and womanly again; who are tired of not being able to keep up with the latest fashion because mutton-dressed lamb is a scream (isn't it?); who's favourite designer is probably Cardin, or Lanvin, or Yves St. Laurent; and who look forward with tears of joy to the return of Molyneaux.

### THEIR YEAR

The Mods see no reason why 1965 isn't going to be as much their year as ever. They have brilliant designing talent, crackling with plenty of new ideas, on their side; they have the formidable economic force of a gigantic young market behind them that certainly isn't interested in trying to look mature and sophisticated and world-weary.

The Elegants can boast some pretty formidable designing talent on their side too; and they too can claim an impressive economic force—the millions of women who have no desire to look kooky and no talent for it.

On their side, too, they feel, is the urge for change which is the basic motive power of fashion—and there are already plenty of signs that things are going their way.

Even Tuffin & Foale say "more elegance, less gimmicks" for 1965; even Mary Quant thinks the 1965 girl will be more streamlined, not so dolly. And James Wedge think that over the next two years, the trend to more expensive clothes, more chic, will have established itself. Women's Wear Daily, the powerful mouthpiece of the great American Rag Trade, has been running its intensive campaign for the Proper Look, the slightly older, more mature, more elegant look or—as they were more deplorably putting it at one time, Le Look Raffine.

THE MOD LOOK : From the Vidal haircut right down to the mod Moya shoes. Model Jan de Souza wears Tuffin & Foale's brand-new trouser suit in black chequered wool ; bigger checks for the jacket, smaller checks for the trousers ; a black, shiny sweater. Tuffin & Foale think trouser suits are great, plan to do plenty more of them in 1965. You can buy all this lot at Top Gear, new Mods' paradise, hole-in-the-wall-sized, in Kings Road,

Barbara Griggs on the Mod Look in the *Evening Standard*, January 1965: 'Model Jan de Souza wears Tuffin and Foale's brand-new trouser suit in black chequered wool; bigger checks for the jacket; smaller checks for the trousers; a black, shiny sweater.'

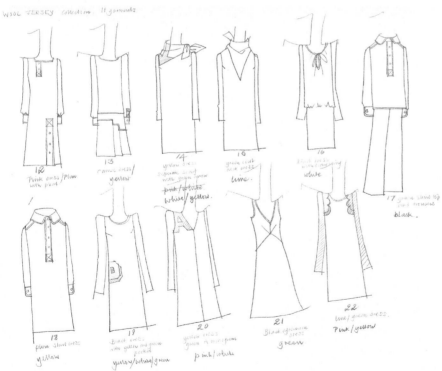

Yardley-sponsored 'Youthquake' fashion show, USA, 1965.

Foale and Tuffin sketches including the D dress, 1966.

**Opposite page:**
Sally (left), John Jesse (right) and James Wedge (back centre) at the opening of Paraphernalia, 1965.

**I opened a stall in Portobello Road** in the summer of 1963, specialising in art nouveau. At that time, my stall was thought to be very cutting edge and kitsch because nouveau was considered by anybody with good taste to be rubbish. However, there was a group of avant-garde people who liked my stall, and among them was an old school friend of mine called Peter Britton. At some point he must have told his flatmate Sally Tuffin, and that is how I came to meet Sally.

My wife Sally had also started a business making ties and handbags, and she used the business name of Sally Jess. The bags were very successful accessories and soon featured in *Vogue*, etc., and sold in many of the same retailers as Foale and Tuffin clothes, such as Woollands. On Saturday afternoons after I had closed up the Portobello stall, Sally T., Marion and her boyfriend Geoffrey Kirkland would hang out with us.

At the same time as running my stall in Portobello Road, I hit on the idea of making shirts in flowered fabrics for men, which at the time was unheard of, as it was such a sissy thing. This was just before Michael Fish set up his shirt business. The label was 'FUNSHIRT'. It seems such an awful name now, but then no one could take them seriously. My wife sold ties made from Liberty's selection of Tana lawn cottons and my shirts were to match them. For my project Sally Tuffin also found some op art fabrics and offered her own factory, Nightstop Productions, to make them. I sold the shirts in Woollands, Liberty and Austin Reed. I am wearing one of those shirts with matching tie in a photograph of Sally and me dancing, which I believe was taken in a New York nightclub in the autumn of 1966. It was reputedly in *Life* magazine. I think it was the long and the short of us that attracted the photographer.

We had gone to New York for the opening of a boutique specialising in British 'Swinging Sixties' fashion. Mary Quant, Moya Bowler, Sally and Marion, Sally Jesse and John somebody or other were the participants. Susannah York opened it. The boutique was called Paraphernalia. I just came along for the ride.

We did socialise a lot, and it being a small world, the Foale and Tuffin shop model was Jenny Boyd (Pattie's sister), who was going out with Mick Fleetwood (the drummer of Fleetwood Mac), who happened to be the brother of my wife Sally.

My wife bought many of their clothes and still probably has some. She also worked for Foale and Tuffin for a while as the manager of their shop. I remember most of all a frock called 'Double Diamond'.

Once when Sally Tuffin was in Tangier on holiday with us, we noticed that there were photos of the King of Morocco in every shop, and Sally T. mentioned in passing that he was quite good-looking. Well, my wife and I thought that he resembled an antique dealer friend of ours and set up a date for them. The man was Richard Dennis and they subsequently married!

Although I wasn't present at the time, I was told a story that Sally T. and Richard were being taken to Claridge's for dinner and Sally was not allowed in because the dress code forbade trouser suits on women. To get round the problem, Sally simply took off the trousers and went into dinner wearing the jacket as a minidress. Sally tells the story differently, but I like the version I was told best.

Foale and Tuffin broke up in the early seventies, as did Sally Jesse and myself. It was the end of an era.

For me Sally and Marion were the epitome of the Swinging Sixties. They were vibrant, alive, cutting edge, adventurous, brilliant designers and incredibly loyal friends – who else would have cheered me up by taking me for a slap-up meal at the Rib Room after my shop was cleared out in a robbery?

# John Jesse

**I always loved their clothes.** I loved them so much that I used to buy the same dress in three or four different colourways. And I wore them for a long time. I liked Foale and Tuffin much better than any of the other designers because their clothes really suited me. Jean Muir was a bit too elegant for me, and I really don't remember wearing much Mary Quant. It was definitely the dresses that I liked; those little minidresses. There was one dress with a geometric pattern that they did in ice-cream colours. It was cut in a crêpey fabric. I think I had that one in every colour they did. I just really liked them.

Up until that period it had been very dour. Everything had been very restrained, and suddenly there was the miniskirt and this explosion of colour and, well, freedom really.

Before I started working the models of the time were rather proper, like Barbara Goalen, all wearing their little white gloves with a handbag and pearls. They were the girls of the moment. But only a year later suddenly it all changed. The beginning of it was definitely David Bailey and Jean Shrimpton. I was still a nobody when they took off. I was quite late on the scene really; I didn't come along until a year or so later. I didn't get off the ground for ages. When I started I used to do show modelling, the catwalk – the girls that do that now are the crème de la crème, but at that time you were the bottom of the pile.

I didn't get picked up until Norman Parkinson spotted me and took a shine to me. He must have come over and had one of his 'cattle markets', when the girls would be lined up and he'd see if there was anyone he liked. I was lucky. He took a fancy to me. So I did a couple of stories for *Queen* magazine when Parkinson first discovered me, and then they put me on a contract for a year. I remember I went straight off to Paris with Parkinson

to photograph the collections, that was with Jocelyn Stevens. Then I worked with other photographers and Parkinson didn't like that. He wanted you all to himself. So he'd drop you.

It really was a wonderful time. We all used to bump into each other all the time because we all went to the same sort of parties – the photographers and models and designers and music business people. Fashion and music especially were so rolled up together. Everybody was having a wonderful time. It was a whole lot of fun, there's no doubt about that. We would be out every night clubbing and I'd bump into Sally and Marion because we went to the same places.

I was having so much fun I never really stopped to analyse things. I didn't really follow fashion that much anyway. At the end of the day I'd just pull on a pair of jeans. Of course, if I went out I did dress up and then more often than not I would wear one of their dresses. I just really liked Foale and Tuffin dresses. They really suited me.

The sixties was a very optimistic period because the late fifties were really very dreary. I remember when I was eighteen or so I was still living at home with my parents, and I wasn't allowed out. I had to explain where I was going. It was very strict and drab. Then the sixties happened and blew all that out of the water. It was a fantastic time and I'm really glad to have lived through it. Everything was new for me. I had such a sheltered upbringing. My life changed completely. I left home and became a swinger and a hippy. It was great, although my mother didn't think so.

# Celia Hammond

# METALCHEMY!
## The new gold and glitter wizardry

King Midas went too far: he meddled in wizardry, wished for gold, and by mistake froze his daughter into a golden girl. The gilded lily here can still dance, and this modern metalchemy has been worked by magical new brocades spilling over into a wild new evening glitter and glow.
**Cloth of gold dress** in Lurex and black glitter, neck and armholes black braided, by Tuffin & Foale, 17 gns., at Woollands; more shops for dress on page 208. Midas touch make-up: Germaine Monteil's Night Light Gold, Revlon's Gold Lamée powder and foundation, or Estée Lauder's Golden Diamond series for skin, lids and lips. Hair style by Raphael & Leonard

**Goldfinger rings:** First finger, a gold dome of diamonds netted in gold, by Kutchinsky, £335. Third finger, diamonds flowerlike in gold, by Kutchinsky, £285. Large gold dome with a wood finish, transversed with double diamonds, by Michael Gosschalk, £300. Fourth finger, two diamond flowers on a gold crossover, by Garrard, £1,025.
**Gold bracelets** glittered with diamonds. Nearest to the hand, domed gold, striped with diamonds, by Boucheron, £1,300. Diamonds in triple rows on gold, by Kutchinsky, £895. Crunchy gold with diamond-centred flowers, by Kutchinsky, £475. Gold watch set squarely in diamonds, by Vacheron et Constantin, £790, at Watches of Switzerland

**Gold sandal** with set-back heel and rhinestone button, Jean Muir's first shoe design, at Rayne, Regent St.; Bond St., end of November.
**The newly minted brocades,** *top to bottom:* Fuchsia brocade with a formal Indian design in different golds, by Abrahams, 36 in., at Liberty. Warm pink cloqué with Eastern tracery, 36 in., 5 gns. a yd., Allans of Duke Street. Pink and gold brocade, by Bianchini, 36 in., Liberty. Gilded brocade with little coloured flowers, by Labbey, 36 in., 5 gns. a yd., Harvey Nichols

DAVID BAILEY

Marion (left) and Sally, 1964,
*Ron Stone/Schroder.*

Clockwise from top left:
Sketch of shift dresses, 1965.
Sketch of jersey vest dresses, 1965.
Sketch of jersey vest dresses, 1965.
Sketch of jersey vest dresses, 1965.

SHIFTY                              2

2 tone cotton Jersey.

Bright Pink / Red.

NO: 3.

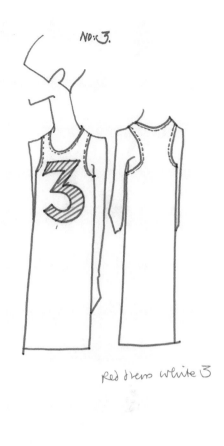

Red dress white 3

QUEEN                              6

Striped cotton Jersey
with Appliqued Heart.

Rayon Jersey Red/White Red Heart
Pink/White Rayon crepe Red Hearts.

LONG JUMP                    2| 3

HIGH JUMP

① Pale blue rayon crepe trimmed with pink.
HARGRD RAYON CREPE.
② BLACK + WHITE TRIM
③ WHITE + PERSIMMON RED TRIM
④ JUBILEE GOLD. + glory blue.

# WE WERE GOING TO BE DIFFERENT

**Foale and Tuffin conversation two**
Iain R. Webb

**When you were at the RCA, you were given a talk by Alexander Plunkett-Green. Was that what made you think you could do something?**

M / It certainly did for me. Yeah. It had a big effect on me. He came to talk about Bazaar, how they set it up, even how they costed things, how it all happened, and you just thought, 'Well, if they can do it just like that …' They didn't know anything about it; they did have Archie McNair though, didn't they? They had an accountant, but you just thought, if they can do it, we can do it.

S / We didn't have an accountant.

M / It really worked for their business, whereas we didn't have any of that, we were just two girls.

**So when you left, what made you join together to start the business?**

S / Well first of all it was the four of us, and then the two of us.

M / Well, we'd been to Walthamstow together, the other two hadn't, I mean we had more of a bond anyway and we just looked at each other and said, 'Let's go it alone.'

S / I think they were thinking a different way, I think we were a bit more rebellious.

M / They weren't as adventurous, they were quite happy to be stuck out in the sticks in Harrow. We wanted to be where it was happening. Stuck out there we'd go to Woolworths and have a tomato soup for lunch, I mean, no, no, no, we wanted to get back to London.

**And your parents gave you sewing machines for your twenty-first birthdays?**

S / Yes.

M / You know that picture of me in front of the machine, that's my sewing machine. 'A sewing machine, a sewing machine, a girl's best friend'.

**So what age were you when you left the RCA?**

M / I was always a year younger than Sally. I'd have probably been twenty-three and Sally would have been twenty-four. It was 1961 when we left the RCA. I was born in 1939; you do the maths.

**And where did you set up together?**

M / First of all we were in my little bed-sit in Brechin Place in Gloucester Road, with another friend living in there as well. Then we went on to Jimmy Wedge's in Westbourne Grove. He had the ground floor, and he had a snooker room and we were in there working on top of the snooker table. That's where we were next and that's where we did the Woollands 21 Shop stuff.

**Were the designs you were doing at college at the end similar to what you were doing when you got out and did your own thing?**

M / First of all when we got out I think we were doing private orders to keep ourselves going. I know I worked with Leslie Poole, to do bridesmaid dresses and things like that. We were still together but obviously looking after ourselves and we'd done our degree shows, which really was not the kind of stuff we started to do afterwards, because that was much more far-fetched. You tried to put almost everything in. We knew how we wanted to dress, which was a much chicer, younger style, whereas we'd done all this flamboyant stuff, clever stuff. Basically we were designing stuff to wear ourselves, really, and we knew that that's what all young people wanted to be wearing. Why would they want to wear this boring old fifties fuddy-duddy look, or even couture come to that? We were into dancing and running around.

**When you came to do those first things for Woollands, were they designed specifically?**

M / I think we did them specifically for them, I think we

thought let's get together a nice little presentation pack and go and show it. I can't remember us thinking to go and show it to anybody else. Why would we? Who was there?

S / We did, because we showed it to Susan Small and she copied that white collar.

M / So maybe we did trot around with it.

S / I think we trotted it around.

M / We did a presentation of the sort of thing we would offer.

S / And the only people that picked it up were, as far as I remember, Woollands.

**And Vanessa at that time was the same sort of age as you?**

M / Yes, it was called timing.

S / It was a lovely store.

**Do you remember going along and seeing her?**

M / Yes, it was pretty easy really, she was looking for it and we'd got it and we wanted to sell it.

S / And we did it all on the shop floor, which you wouldn't do now. We'd show up at the shop with the things over our arms and we'd show them to her and she'd say 'Oh, yes, that's lovely I'll have three of those' and we'd go back on the bus and make three.

M / There was no offices or delivering to offices or 'round the back', you delivered into the shop. I can remember being on the shop floor with stuff.

**Had you set up as Foale and Tuffin Ltd then?**

M / Had we? I can't remember when we did that exactly.

S / Yeah, I remember the Royal College's accountant became ours, he was obviously used to this, people leaving college and needing help, and he must have just said this is the package that we do.

### Was that when you created your logo?

s / No, just after then.

m / Well, it got serious and then it had to be done.

s / We got David Cripps to design it.

m / Yes, David Cripps. He went to college with us; we were all in the same group. He used to go out with Pauline Boty, and then after she died he went out with Janice Wainwright and they got married.

s / I went to Spain with him and Pauline, my boyfriend and I, and all these people were standing and looking at them, so I said, 'What's everybody looking at us for?' and David said, 'because we are so beautiful!', and he and she were, they were absolutely stunning. She was like Bardot.

### You took your stuff to Woollands, one of which was the grey dress with the white frill front.

m / Well she picked two and we delivered three of each and she put one of each in the window, and then Claire Rendlesham from *Vogue* came along, saw them and said, 'I'll have that. I'll photograph that' and then David Bailey, this new young photographer took a photograph.

### And how did that feel?

m / Well, it was very nice.

s / I think we were quite casual about it. We just thought that's what happens when you are a dress designer from the Royal College, but really we were just so lucky.

m / We were. Again it was just timing and it was meant to be, and they were looking for somebody to be doing it and there it was. Then they need thirty-six of each style, and so on. And then we found out it's an awful lot of hard work cutting out thirty-six of each style, and the sewing up, so then we progressed to finding a lady to sew, we pressed the dresses ourselves and we delivered them ourselves but then it gradually

progressed from that; new styles and another range. It was just a progression then.

### On your letterhead there is another name?

s / John Stitt? He came to us when we were doing pretty well from the bank and decided that he would be involved with us and guide us into better things. He didn't understand us at all. I think it was the perfect example of when the accountants start coming into a fashion house, and we must have realised that and backed out, but I don't remember. I didn't know he was a director, that's interesting.

m / No, I can't remember that at all, but I know exactly who you mean.

### You were basically looking after everything. Had you been trained in that or was it something you had to pick up as you went along?

m / Buying the fabric, checking the patterns, grading. We had been trained to make complete patterns and to make a garment from scratch, with a bit of brown paper, or on the stand, so we just did everything from scratch.

### And the business side?

m / We knew nothing about it. We just did it.

s / It sort of happened.

### And being two young women at that time?

s / Actually it wasn't difficult.

m / We just did it.

s / We were able to go to the clubs we wanted to go to, buy the shoes we wanted to, we made our own clothes, we led a pretty comfortable life.

m / We went to get the bolts of fabric, and OK, it was usually men in grey suits that used to go to buy fabric, but they thought it was so funny that they let us do it. Off we went with grey flannel and red flannel over our shoulders.

s / Maybe just bravado and ignorance.

### You actually bought fabric direct from Bourne & Hollingsworth and Liberty and ...

s / m / Dickins & Jones.

### At retail price?

m / Yes.

s / But we picked odd things like nun's veiling, things that you didn't normally buy, we researched odd things. I think we were just drawn to being contrary.

m / And we were drawn to it because it was different. We were going to be different.

### Who was your competition at that time?

s / Well, there was Mary, wasn't there.

m / Mary Quant and there wasn't really anybody else.

s / No, Jean Muir hadn't started.

m / She was still at Jaeger or wherever she was.

s / There wasn't Zandra, there wasn't even Biba.

m / There wasn't really, but they soon started to follow on.

### So what was the path you took to get to your own boutique?

s / A phone call from Jimmy Wedge saying, 'There is an office free in Carnaby Street. Do you want it? I'm moving out.' And it was six and a half guineas a week. So we said, 'Yes'. That was on the first floor at Marlborough Court, and there was a shop below, and when the shop became vacant we took it and that was the beginning.

m / There was a telephone box on the alleyway.

### What sort of timing is that?

s / I suppose that was, oh gosh, it was about the time that Marit got married.

m / What was that, '65-ish?

s / I think so.

### When you got there what was the look you wanted?

m / We had to cover up a very ugly wall so we got a Casa Pupo rug, a black and white rug, and we were thrilled to bits to have our own little office to work in.

I don't think we even had the shop when The Beatles came in, did we, because they came upstairs. So we were there for quite a bit selling wholesale.

**S /** We were in two rooms, front and back.

**M /** Yes, but at the same time the American thing had already set off and I think Paul Young had found us, because we were going backwards and forwards. We'd been over with suitcases and the Americans had found us, and I remember that Sally Kirkland came over to interview us in that office. We didn't have the shop then, and then we did get the shop, but not as a shop – we used it as a showroom. We had a green felt screen which we put 'Chosen by *Vogue*' pictures on.

**S /** And we had a 'man wall' at the back, didn't we?

**M /** Yes.

**S /** With all our favourite men on.

**M /** And we used it as an office and we did sewing upstairs, I think, before it even became a shop, and then we were kind of bamboozled into a shop because the Americans were really coming on strong and heavy, and the whole thing was breaking out and people wanted 'Swinging Sixties' and we thought, well, we might as well open a shop!

**S /** None of the retailers minded, it was extraordinary. Then James opened Top Gear in the Kings Road and then Countdown. He was a pretty good buyer. And then there was Browns.

### Were you selling the same things that you had in your shop?

**M /** Yes, we just showed the whole range, and by then we were using a factory just outside Clapham. They took us on and they were very good.

**S /** They were called Nightstop Productions.

**M /** And we stuck with them for years actually and they were really good.

### So you could turn things around quickly?

**S /** Yes, it was pretty quick. You'd give them an order, the cloth, the pattern and the order sheets, the deliveryman would take them one week and he would bring them back the next week

**M /** And then we had to find a tailoring factory as well, so that was the Redum Brothers in the East End. That was typical, real Jewish, proper Jewish tailors.

### When you moved into your boutique what was the interior like?

**M /** We started off with the light bulbs didn't we?

**S /** It was a small space, and to get the maximum out of the space we just put scaffolding poles right across widthways and then hung the hangers on those. The shop was designed by the jeweller Tony Laws.

**M /** And the hangers had to have long bits. They were so high up that we could walk underneath but they had to be long so you could actually reach them and see the clothes.

**S /** And all around above those were the light bulbs, blue and red light bulbs.

**M /** And we had two changing rooms, two white curtained corners.

**S /** And minimal wooden floor and minimal white desk. That's it. Oh, and a model of Twiggy in the window. The window went straight to the floor and there would just be Twiggy standing in all sorts of poses.

### A mannequin?

**S /** Yes, which we left when we left, which is a shame.

**M /** It was an Adel Rootstein [mannequin designer].

### So you were working upstairs?

**M /** Yes, but then we got Ganton Street as well at that point.

**S /** We were working upstairs, because I remember working away and getting a phone call from the shop, from Acushla, saying there is someone down here who needs to see you,

and it was Jo Bergman in the changing room – and Jo was a funny shape, she's a bit like Mae West, she was stuck in a dress and she just said 'Help!' She was such a wonderful character, and she came regularly after that. Every collection, she would order.

### Between Woollands and the boutique, talk me through the American thing.

**S /** They'd found us.

**M /** Was it *Life* magazine, there was a big article and there was a whole thing on 'Youthquake'?

**S /** Or *Time*, or *Time Life* or whatever.

**M /** Also we were doing whistle-stop tours by then. We were going to America doing 'Youthquake', which meant we were doing whistle-stop tours from city to city, and you'd get there in the morning and you'd have to do breakfast TV, and we were like 'God what's that supposed to be?', we'd never heard of it. So you were straight on, they wanted you to get up and dance at breakfast time and show them how to do it, and then you went into the store and you gave a dress show. We had a catwalk and go-go girls and the Skunks doing the music, and then in the evening they'd give you dinner and you'd be absolutely shattered and you'd finally get to bed then have to get up early to get the next plane to the next city. It was big in the States.

**S /** I think they picked us because somebody like *The Times* did an article about the 'young somethings'.

### And who took you over there?

**S /** We took ourselves

**M /** But we were found by Paul Young.

**S /** But we had the sense to stay in the Algonquin, I mean we were quite clued up really.

**M /** I think it's just because we liked everything nice. We liked to do it in style.

**S /** No, we had been to America before Paul Young.

**M /** Yes, we had because we took the suitcases.

**S /** And then I think it was Sally Kirkland who picked us up and Ossie [Clark] and John Kloss, and Baby Jane Holzer decided she quite liked what we did.

**M /** And then this guy came along and he wanted to do a whole big thing with Mary Quant, Betsey Johnson and us, and that's when the whistle-stop tours were. His name was Paul Young and he was affiliated to Puritan Fashions Corporation, and it was called 'Youthquake' and it came under another section, Paraphernalia. They manufactured under that name – some of our garments actually have one of our labels, and then tacked on to it you might find a Paraphernalia label as well.

**S /** There was a boutique on Madison Avenue because Susannah York came and opened it for Paul Young and he gave her loads of clothes.

**M /** That must have been about the time of doing Kaleidoscope, the Warren Beatty and Susannah York film.

### So all of these things happened incredibly quickly. It was a whirlwind affair?

**M /** It was fast. It was like, hang on here, let's have a good night's sleep and a breather, but no it was just … but that's how it always is.

**S /** Wasn't it you that was frightened of flying, or was that Pru?

**M /** Don't think that was me because I've never minded flying. I think it must have been Pru, she was one of the go-go dancers, she was the wife of our roadie, I mean it is funny isn't it?

### You were like a band on tour.

**M /** Well, it was really. I think it's brilliant that we had the Skunks. It really topped it off.

**S /** They had bleached hair

**M /** But to say you'd got your own group for your catwalk show with your go-go girls. People loved it.

**S /** And the women from the shops who were our hostesses

when they went home they'd change into their normal clothes
**M** / They didn't know how to wear them.
**s** / They weren't 'with it' at all! They didn't like it really.
**M** / It was hilarious because they didn't understand any of it.
**s** / And there they were selling it.
**M** / They had it all hanging up there and we'd just think, well what's going to happen with all this stuff?
**s** / Americans being American.
**M** / I've got to do this, got to jump on this bandwagon.
**s** / Very generously, they put their money where their mouths were, but somehow you'd feel it wasn't really something they liked, probably.
**M** / But then later I met someone who said he used to be at Saks when all that was happening and he said, 'Why didn't you guys make a killing? You should be so wealthy and made a killing on it, and you didn't!'
**s** / I think that's why that accountant came on-board, because I think he realised that as well.
**M** / We never did make the killing.

**But very few of those businesses did.**

**M** / It wasn't what we were out to be doing anyway, we were out to be doing what we wanted to do and not what they wanted us to do.
**s** / But I think we made a contribution to fashion, I think we had an influence, and I do remember taking the 'Fringed Collection' to France. We were doing quite well with Dorothée Bis, a small boutique on the Left Bank and she said, 'Oh, no no, you can't do fringing, everyone will think you're a prostitute if you wear fringing'. She wouldn't buy it, and that same year Saint Laurent did the same thing and everybody was like, 'Wow'. I think the whole of London did quite a lot at that time to stir things up, because previously to that Italy was the place, everything was coming from Italy.

**M** / Well, that and couture. Paris really was very important.
**s** / But really things were happening in Italy, if you had a choice.
**M** / They were doing nice knitwear in Italy, it was really good.
**s** / Wonderful shoes.
**M** / Nice colours.

**You mentioned the 'Swinging London' thing; there is that Parkinson photograph of you all on the lamp post by the Thames. What was that taken for?**

**M** / For an American magazine. It was [Norman] Parkinson's photograph and I think it was for *Life* magazine, *Time Life* magazine.
**s** / I think it was.
**M** / I think it was all part of that.

**And did you feel part of a group?**

**M** / Yes, we were doing what was wanted and now there were more people doing it.
**s** / So it was fun and that shoot was particularly fun. It was wonderful.
**M** / Yes it was.
**s** / We all went to the pub afterwards. It was a lovely day.

**And you all got on?**

**s** / Yes, we did actually. Back then there wasn't fashion 'bitching'.
**M** / I think we all just thought how lucky we were.
**s** / Yes, or we were just naive. I think we were just naive.
**M** / I think we just went for it.
**s** / We were aware that you had to hide your offcuts when you were doing samples.
**M** / So that nobody found it and could see what you were doing.
**s** / Also things were beginning to be stolen at the factories. a whole collection would be stolen. It was all still a bit ad hoc, even the buying process, you know, Mrs Burstein would come and sit on the sofa and it would be a laugh and giggle.
**M** / She'd bring her two children with her.
**s** / And Jimmy Wedge would come with Pat Booth and she'd be naughty. It was lovely.

**M** / Pauline Denyer was with us at that point. She used to model as well. She went to the Royal College with us but she was younger than us and she had her babies early. So when she left the RCA she needed work, and she came and did sample machining and grading. Oh, was it after Westbourne Grove we went to your flat in Gloucester Walk?
**s** / I think so.
**M** / So it was Brechin Place first for a very short time on the dining table, then it was Westbourne Grove and then it was Gloucester Walk, where Sally had a big flat, and Marit and Caterine Milinaire came there to see the collection. I can remember it was that freezing cold winter.

**So you were saying about Susannah York and the film. So Marit got you to do things for the film?**

**M** / Yes. Maybe they went to *Vogue* and said who would you suggest and they said, 'Marit Allen – sort this out!'
**s** / Yes, I think that was it.

**So was the 'Kaleidoscope' collection for the film?**

**M** / Yes, I can't remember how many things we did.

**So did you go out when the film was made?**

**M** / We flew to St-Tropez and sitting in front of us was Rudolf Nureyev.
**s** / No, no, no it wasn't St-Tropez.
**M** / Nice?
**s** / Monte Carlo.
**M** / I know we went to Monte Carlo but we flew to Nice, which is the nearest airport. Nice anyway, Rudolf Nureyev was sitting in front or behind.
**s** / And we stayed in the same hotel.
**M** / Yes, and it was that really smart hotel opposite the casino, and we actually went to the casino one night, then you'd sit in this grand restaurant in the evening.
**s** / It was lovely.

**M /** Yes, and in the bedrooms we had white towelling robes.

### How were you both dressed at that time?

**S /** We were wearing what Susannah was wearing in the film.

**M /** We were probably wearing those jersey dresses with zips at that point; I think we might have been into the 'jersey phase' and jackets as well.

**S /** Those shaped jackets.

**M /** We weren't into the pretty prints yet, that hadn't started.

**S /** It was all quite basic, it was …

**M /** Clean. Clean design.

**S /** And for the first night of the film in London we hired a painted stretch limo all the colours of the rainbow. And we must have worn all the lime greens and the oranges and stuff that went with it. I've still got a ticket for it; I found it upstairs, it's lovely.

**M /** Absolutely brilliant, gosh, that stretch limo! I'd seen it driving around London and I tracked it down and said we have to go in that! And we did, and everybody was looking. It was great.

### So Monte Carlo was where filming was being done?

**M /** Yes. They were filming there. We were actually on set to help with Susannah's clothes, maybe if they needed a tweak here and there, and dress her and this, that, and the other. And we went to rushes and Warren Beatty came up to us and said, 'I love your clothes you did for the film.'

### So you were leading very glamorous lives?

**M /** Yes, we were very lucky.

### Especially as young women coming from relatively humble backgrounds?

**M /** And we knew a lot of people in that whole era like Ridley Scott, Tom Stoppard and Ridley Scott's friend Geoffrey Kirkland, who does the sets for Alan Parker.

**S /** We were doing better than Tom because I remember buying champagne when his first child was born.

**M /** And Ridley Scott was only just starting; we were before him, and his brother Tony.

### Was he doing commercials then?

**M /** He was doing commercials and Geoffrey Kirkland was doing *The Likely Lads*. He was my 'fella'. He was production designer for *The Likely Lads* and I was living with him at that point, and before we were living together Geoffrey and Ridley were living together.

**S /** And Peter Tebbitt was Rodney Bewes' wife's brother.

### The photographer?

**S /** So that was another group we would party with.

**M /** The two writers we got on really well with, Ian La Frenais and Dick Clement. They always used to hang out after the show, they were always around.

### Quite crazy. And The Beatles as well?

**S /** And the Rolling Stones. Jo Bergman was the Rolling Stones' PA, so we used to go and sit about that far from them when they were performing.

**M /** And I remember she rented out my flat to them as well.

### So you would go and see them perform and then they would come to your boutique?

**S /** I don't think the Stones ever bought from us.

**M /** But I remember going to a private rehearsal in Wardour Street in the middle of the afternoon.

**S /** And, of course, we were also connected with the pop artists at the time.

**M /** Yes.

**S /** It was pop music, pop artists, TV, film, the whole thing.

### And all new and all happening at that time with young people?

**M /** Zandra Rhodes' first job was with us, that's how she started. We were still on our one floor above at Marlborough Court, and she'd left college after us

and came to us and wanted to sell her prints to people that made clothes, and she couldn't, and could we look at them and could we use them, and we did. We went on with that until she felt that she wanted us to do the designs of the garments as she wanted them designed and we said perhaps it's time for you to do it yourself. So she went to work with Sylvia Ayton.

**S /** But the first time she came with her prints, she came with a big piece of paper with a hole in the top and she just put it over her head.

**M /** And it fitted.

**S /** And she had filthy hands, didn't she?

**M /** From all the printing.

**S /** We did quite a lot with her.

**M /** That photograph of Janey [Best] wearing the star print, which was taken by Janey's brother. That was a Zandra Rhodes print.

**S /** And there were domino prints, but we didn't go big on her banana men and lipstick prints.

**M /** But she did much better for going off with Sylvia than she would have ever done with us, so it was the right way for it to happen.

### The look in the beginning was that very simple, little girl look.

**M /** And we used to borrow a lot of military ideas, didn't we? We had gold braid.

### And the double-breasted jacket.

**M /** And good buttons, like forces' buttons.

### The little girl thing was coming out of 'Mod'?

**M /** Yes, 'Mod'.

**S /** 'Mod'. Yes. The Beatles were 'Mod', weren't they?

### Was it in part thinking, 'This is what we can do and we can turn these out' or was it that this was the look that you created because you wanted to wear it?

**M /** Yes [the latter].

**S /** We were never commercial.

**M /** No never. If we didn't want to wear it we wouldn't do it. If we didn't like it we wouldn't do it. End of story.

**S /** The nearest thing we got to commercialism was when we decided that two and a half yards was the maximum we should spend on a blouse.

### What was your look at that time? Was that when you had your bob hairdos? Who cut those?

**S /** Vidal or Christopher Brooker. The bob man.

### And that's when you did that photograph of the two of you?

**M /** Yes. The David Montgomery.

### And that became the drawing as well?

**S /** Yes.

### It was a very graphic look, I suppose that came from pop art?

**S /** And pop art came from that feel as well, because just before then, what was happening before pop art at the Royal College? Oh I know, that 'kitchen sinky' sort of look.

**M /** Stark realism. Brutal realism.

### And then it suddenly became graphic and colourful and inspired by modern culture. It was very much about modernity at that time. Looking to the future, looking to something very optimistic.

**M /** And you were definitely looking forward and not looking back. There was nothing fuddy-duddy and fifties. It was all new, new, new.

**S /** You weren't even aware of the problem of the atom bomb. That had happened more in the fifties, that dreadful Australian film, *On the Beach*. But somehow in the sixties you weren't aware of any impending big problem, and even the smaller wars that were happening didn't affect us, did it?

**M /** No, we just blindly carried on.

**And also you had escaped your backgrounds?**

M / Yes.
s / But ironically we didn't do drugs. We were just before that.
M / We were lucky.
s / We certainly did alcohol but we didn't do drugs. We did like the odd brandy and coke.
M / Rum and coke. Whisky mac. Whisky mac was a big one.
s / And we did smoke cigarettes, I think.
M / Oh yes, we did, we sure did.
s / Of course we did. So we were quite lucky we kept our wits about us.

**Now lets talk about all the fabulous girls you dressed, like Marianne Faithfull. You went from doing something graphic and simple to something very pretty, the frills, the pretty prints.**

M / Then it went hippy.
s / Flower Power.
M / We were into the flower thing, the hippy thing. People were LSDing, they were beginning to do all of that, that was 1967, '68, when all of that burst on to the scene.
s / Oh that's right, because I met Richard [Dennis] in 1967 and went to Egypt and came back with loads of kaftans and things.

**The whole ethnic thing.**

M / The summer of Flower Power.
s / But before we were putting flower prints together.

**Before that you did the Jane Asher thing, which was quite early on, and that was the little Liberty prints, and quite sweet looking.**

s / Yes, they were flowers weren't they? Liberty prints and lace.

**Did you feel amongst all this modernity you wanted a bit of romance?**

M / I think we wanted to be feminine and a little bit pretty, but it was still within the parameters of a very clean look.

s / And we'd go into Liberty's, and you saw this blue and white fabric and thought, 'yes, that's so fresh and lovely', then you have to cut according to your cloth. You have to make something that suits that.

**So the same simplicity, but with a softer edge than before.**

s / And then of course we got into the Liberty voiles, so we did floppy things. So fabric led the way, I think.
M / And also in Broadwick Street there was a lace shop, and we saw the lace in there and suddenly you're inspired. It was actually more inspired by fabrics, instead of dreaming up the fabric – we'll go and get nun's veiling, or grey flannel, or Dormeuil …
s / But you can't do that after a while, it just becomes so boring, you have to move on. On reflection, we were so starved of anything to really work with, there was nothing about, and that's why we finished up in Liberty because at least then you had a good quality product, good colour.
M / And then to think about quilting it. It was something that nobody had ever done.
s / Or we made them do a bright blue colourway. They didn't do bright blue but we made them do it, and things like that, to get a bit of 'oomph' going.

**So you then picked from ranges by people like Bernard Nevill and Susan Collier? They inspired you?**

s / Yes. Or you knew you were going to do a kaftan so you could use a bigger print, and at that stage Nevill had a wonderful big flower thing in subtle shades.

**He went through his 'country phase', gardens and jazzy prints.**

s / Yes. And of course we were just around the corner from there.
M / And there were all these beautiful paisleys as well.
s / Oh my God, yes, the paisleys.
M / The paisleys were just 'Wow!'
s / I think that's why we started to go to Liberty's, because from

'tartany' things we went into paisley things.
M / Yes, traditional.
s / Because we were buying old paisley shawls and that might have triggered that off.
M / Yes, because we were quite traditional in our fabrics to begin with, and maybe we then progressed to paisley, which was traditional, and then you see all these other goodies, well, even the lace was traditional, very traditional but gorgeous.
s / Because coincidentally we were buying old patchwork quilts and paisley shawls.

**You mentioned going to Egypt. There was this whole thing of the 'hippy trail', or people starting to travel and going to explore the world. Suddenly there was this whole world opening up to you.**

M / Yes.
s / Yes.
M / And to everybody.
s / People like Thea Porter did that beautifully, we didn't do it in that way. We slightly bastardized the whole thing and used it as a fashion influence.
M / Whereas she actually really did it.

**So when you did the quilting thing, it's interesting how people interpret it: you have the *Nova* pictures, where's it's gypsy and then the *Harpers & Queen* pictures, which are oriental. What were you thinking when you designed those things?**

s / There was definitely a Japanese influence there.
M / I think you just feel the inspiration that's around you. You pick up on any inspiration that's happening at the time. Maybe there was an exhibition or something.
s / There was the Klimt exhibition that I remember being very influential on putting things together. I loved to see the Klimts, not that we succeeded in really doing Klimt, but coincidentally a few years ago

we did some Klimt vases here and they just fell off the shelves. But when we quilted these two fabrics together, and I don't know why we did do it, we were aware that then you had a cloth that you were able to mould into shapes, and that would stand up on its own.

**M** / And tailor it.

**S** / So it was like a sort of soft tailoring which people were slightly ready for, more than the structured tailoring. It was a handy thing to use.

**M** / Hippy tailoring, it was more hippy tailoring. Relaxed tailoring, fun casual tailoring instead of all the formal jacket, suit jacket type looks.

**I was talking to Vanessa [Denza] about how you went from one look to another, and it is quite extreme when you look from the very beginning to the end. She said the one thing she felt was that you were always on the button, you always got it right, or you were ahead of your time. Why or how do you think that was the case?**

**M** / It's what's in the air; it's grabbing hold of what's in the air.

**S** / I think it's who you party with, who you talk to.

**M** / And what you're looking at. What exhibitions you're going to.

**S** / You know David Cripps was the art director of the *Observer*, there were architects, there were pop painters, all of whom are now famous, models, very interesting models, musicians and a few writers. So I suppose you just perhaps went to the right clubs, but then the clubs weren't exactly leading fashion.

**M** / No, they weren't, you didn't pick up any ideas from anything like that.

**S** / It could be that you were trained to look at college. Seven years is a very long time to be at art school, and you were trained to use your eyes and receive things.

**M** / That is exactly how it felt. Your eyes are just opened and you can receive.

**S** / Often I can be doing something and I go down a

route and I look at it and I think 'Why on earth? What made me do that?' It wasn't what I intended, but it's just like being channelled through.

**M** / We did look at a lot of movie books.

**S** / Oh yes.

**M** / Old films.

**S** / And new films, Bergman films.

**M** / We were into films big time, clothing in films as well.

**You went through a very definite thirties decadent period as well.**

**M** / Yes.

**S** / Yes. That was probably from old films.

**M** / But it's always that feeling of the moment, that's what people are feeling and wanting, that's why you looked at it. It's just instinct, isn't it?

**I think it is that training of keeping your eyes open.**

**S** / Being able to assimilate everything.

**The changing was quite constant as well. Was that because once you have done something you have to move on to the next thing? Is it a boredom threshold?**

**S** / It was the thought that you had to do a new collection twice a year.

**M** / That's what you've got to do.

**S** / You've got to think new twice a year.

**M** / It was constantly new, new, new.

**I remember reading Twiggy's biography, in which she talks of being a 'Mod' and how literally you had to be on it or you were out of it.**

**M** / That's right. Which length skirt are we on now?

**S** / I remember coming back from the factory, taking all our clothes off and completely changing because that's what you had to wear.

**M** / You couldn't wait.

**S** / You just couldn't face that old-fashioned thing that you put on this morning.

**M** / Fortunately nowadays we can wear anything we like.

**S** / I remember when we stopped, the luxury of being able to go shopping and go even to other people's shops and buy things without feeling guilty.

**Vanessa mentioned you would be walking up and down Carnaby Street in your gear that you were designing and getting attention. You did live and breathe it?**

**M** / Yes, because it was new and it was the right thing to wear that week.

**S** / But we weren't aware of marketing or any of those tricks that you can do, although presumably going to nightclubs and wearing the clothes was doing just that, but we weren't aware of it. And I remember that hairdresser Leonard took us out to lunch, and was awfully nice to us and decided he'd like to cut our hair, and we were quite innocently, 'OK, we'll have our hair cut' but it would never have occurred to us to have done that the other way around. No.

**But were the Y-front dresses and the ones that spelt out J-U-L-I-E [worn by Julie Christie] done because you thought they would have an effect?**

**S** / It was the time of the Olympics.

**M** / It was all sportswear.

**S** / And people were wearing little vests with a band of colour, so we took that idea into dresses.

**And sportswear moved into workwear.**

**M** / I remember Geoffrey had gone over to the States and he had come back, and I was living with him at the time and he had a denim jacket, and the complete thing I knocked off from it called 'Geoff's Jacket' – it's a denim jacket with white stitching and four pockets and that really just started a whole feeling for it, and then it went on to cowboys.

**A whole 'western look'?**

**M** / Yes.

**S** / And the jeans we bought were hipsters, weren't they? I remember going into a big shop in America where they had walls and walls of jeans, which we'd never seen before, and you just stood there and they'd know your size. They'd say, 'button or zip?' and we'd say 'button' and they just went up, got them down. I've still got them, can't get into them now. It was amazing. Absolutely amazing, wasn't it?

**M** / Yes it was.

**S** / And that must have influenced us a lot, and I remember we were wearing jeans and shirts, or jeans and funny little jackets all the time, long before this thing where now everyone wears jeans with everything. So it was a precious thing to do then, an unusual thing to do, so it must have been workwear from America.

**M** / I remember when we went over, we used to actually make a point of looking at the workwear, at the dungarees.

**S** / That's right, the dungarees.

**M** / And all the stitching, and the different fitments like the D-ring things and all the different studs, so I remember we actually studied it, looked at it, and saw all their bits and pieces, and then we'd have to source them in England, the D-rings and what have you. But we definitely looked at workwear and looked at dungarees and denim jackets.

**You dressed an incredible array of girls in the sixties – Twiggy, Jane Asher, Julie Christie, Susannah York, Penelope Tree. Were they people who were around?**

**M** / Marit did a story on Jane Asher and she gave her various clothes to wear. Twiggy and people I think just wanted the clothes; it was what they would wear.

**And Cathy McGowan. In From 'A To Biba', Barbara [Hulanicki] says she watched 'Ready Steady Go!' to see if she was wearing one of her dresses or one of yours. What was the whole thing like?**

M / Exciting!
s / She came to be dressed, I think, and then we were able to go to the shows which was lovely.

**A trade-off.**

M / Dusty Springfield and P. J. Proby. Yeah, it was good fun to actually go, to get a ticket to go.

**You said you were designing for yourselves but were those girls the epitome of the kind of girls you wanted to wear your clothes?**

M / We were all of the same ilk.
s / Yeah, she had the heavy fringe, the straight hair and she wore those little very simple shifty things. Of course the shift must have come from The Sack.
M / Le Sack, from Balenciaga
s / Was it Balenciaga or was it Dior?
M / Balenciaga.

**Do you think that because those girls were all doing something, that influenced you as well to design for a life choice?**

s / Yes, a lifestyle, definitely.
M / Yes …
s / It definitely wasn't for the mum at home.
M / To be part of that whole scene, and exciting and young and buzzy, yes.
s / And remember there were no small clothes available at all. There was nothing like tights, or anything like we take for granted now.

**When you think about fashion history you think the 1960s – OK, Mary Quant and Bazaar and miniskirts, but when it first opened it was those big fifties skirts and still within that era. But actually the change was quite dramatic when it did happen.**

M / It was, yes.
s / But there was Bazaar in the Kings Road and next to it was a coffee bar. A coffee bar was very, very new, very, very modern – you'd go and meet in this coffee bar.
M / And wasn't the Markham pub opposite?
s / I don't remember a pub, Marion.
M / Well, you ought to.
s / And so Mary was on the corner and then beside Mary was Aage Thaarup, the Queen Mother's milliner, and below them was a restaurant that Plunkett-Green opened,

**Talking about the girls. Do you think part of your success was that you were women designing for women?**

M / Yes. I think so.
s / Yes. And bought by women. The retail shops were run by women, which again was probably quite unusual.
M / Women buyers.

**Certainly their youthfulness was new; I think Vanessa was the youngest buyer. So it is really crucial to your success that you were designing for yourselves.**

M / We weren't being commercial and going for the market. I think we were designing for women for themselves, instead of for women dressing to please men. I think that was the difference.
s / And it wasn't clothes to go to a party in, it wasn't clothes to get married in, it was just everyday clothing.
M / And it was for women. Sally – We are basically very, very practical people. We are quite mathematical and we are quite practical.
M / We are, yes.
s / Which presumably came out in the ranges.

**It shifted from 'Design an outfit for tea at so-and-so' or 'Design pyjamas for a teenage sister', that you were doing at the Royal, what women still call 'occasion dressing'. They were being designed for specific occasions**

because at that time, you probably changed throughout the day to fit this or that whereas, as you say, these were clothes that were actually for every day.

M / Yes.
s / Yes.

**And just to get on and live in.**

M / Just to get on, yes, to go to work in and then actually go out in the same.
s / And you could go to a dance in, which was important, although the clothes didn't move very well. The Royal College had a dance every Saturday.
M / Yes. I don't know if it was Saturdays but I know it was every week.
s / In their common room. Or was it Friday night?
M / Friday nights it was, yes.
s / So you'd go to the common room and dance, and they'd have the Temperance Seven there and it was always live music. You were very aware of what was happening to music, and then when the twist came in …
M / Yes! That was interesting.
s / That was one of the funnier eras.
M / And that was one of the things when we were doing our whistle-stop tours in America, on breakfast TV, they made us stand up and show them how to do the twist. It was the most embarrassing thing I've ever done in my life.
s / Oh yes. Ugh!
M / First thing in the morning, you've come off a flight, you're dead tired and they want you to stand up and do the twist. Cold! Most embarrassing thing in the world.

**There was so much you were experiencing that was completely new.**

**M** / Yes.

**S** / And we had nothing to back it up. We hadn't even done a dress show before, do you realise that?

**M** / Yes, I know, we'd never done a proper catwalk.

**S** / We didn't do dress shows, so when we were taken to New York to do catwalk it was our first, whereas I think Mary was quite used to it. Although we did go to a Kansai Yamamoto show, wonderful dress shows he did.

**M** / Yes! He was a good designer.

**S** / I loved those shows. I think that was probably part of why we did Japanese things; I think that was what got us excited about it.

**M** / Yes, I think you're right actually, that's where it could have come from and also we loved kimonos.

143

Opposite page:
Lace-up shift dress, 1964,
*Peter Atherton.*

Foale and Tuffin sketches for
Western-inspired designs, 1966.

NEEDLECHORD Sports Collection. 11 garments.

'Roulette chip' invitation for
*Kaleidoscope* film premiere, 1966.

**Opposite page:**
Susannah York models pink
and silver lurex tweed evening
dress, with *Kaleidoscope* co-star
Warren Beatty, June 1966 *David
Montgomery/Vogue © The Condé
Nast Publications Ltd.*

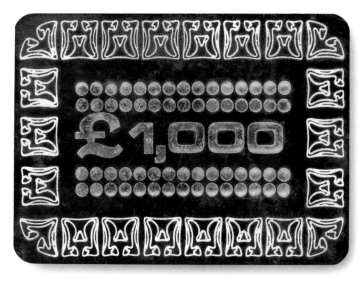

absolutely focussed on one street that none of us more sedate types had ever even heard of. I didn't know where Carnaby Street was. I thought it had a barber there or something and then suddenly the whole street was 'how time' and it was really exciting with all these wonderful talented people breaking into the scene. And there were these two, Foale and Tuffin.

It was the era of the girlies really. There was Foale and Tuffin, there was Mary Quant, Twiggy, Barbara Hulanicki doing Biba, Jean Muir. It was the era of the little dress, and they were little dresses designed for girlies by girlies. Little dresses mostly with bare arms and bare knees. They were intensely feminine. This new school of fashion designers didn't do very much in terms of knock-your-eye-out couture, but they made the girlie look her girlie best in her frock, and these two were just wonderful at it. It was the era of not-the-little-black-dress. It was the little dress that was anything but black. It was also a time when anything would do so long as it wasn't plain. It was a time for sparkle and pattern and colour. I mean colour exploded in a way that one had never seen before – never, never, never – and these two brought such imagination to fashion.

Foale and Tuffin used their fabrics almost as a canvas, like an artist would. They were working with shapes on a flat surface. They would add embellishment, almost drawing and painting objects on to the dresses like signposts. They were like graphic artists. It was very graphic and simple in the same way that the artist Mondrian worked, and that Yves Saint Laurent did later.

They also made Liberty prints into an ultra-modern fabric, and what a miracle that was. Before that, Liberty prints were what upper-class ladies had made into shirts by their dressmaker, and sometimes they had the skirt to match, but these two used it as though it was a revolutionary fabric, they gave it a whole new life. It had never been in the realms of fashion before; it was always very beautiful but very dignified and sophisticated and not for the young, but suddenly Foale and Tuffin were using it for the most modern shapes and silhouettes, really innovative.

What happened is that street fashion met high fashion fabrics, and it made a marriage that had not been seen previously. Fabrics that couture house would use, like those fabulous Bernard Nevill prints, and he was suddenly creating for the street, so these wonderful fabrics were given a whole new lease of life. He was designing, collaborating with these upstart designers. I hope they won't mind me calling them that?

Foale and Tuffin *were* rebels. They really did things that made people sit up, but it worked. They had such talent. And if ever designers wore their own designs wonderfully well, these two did it. They really looked like fashion drawings – they had the figures, they had the faces, they had the hairstyles. They were typical of their time in every possible way. They lived the life, they looked the life, they were the life. They were absolutely the perfect advertisement. This was what it was all about and why it worked so well – they designed it, they were wearing it, they made it come alive.

I had great freedom as associate editor on the *Daily Mirror* newspaper. The Editorial Director, Hugh Cudlipp, gave me the opportunity to feature all the fashions that were new and exciting. I remember he said to me: 'I've not the faintest idea what you're doing but I trust you, don't make us a laughing stock!' So I really had the freedom to put in the paper every week what I thought was news at that time, and it was also the first time I brought proper fashion photographers into the *Mirror*. We didn't have to have the lovely chap who did football matches on Wednesday and fashion on Thursday. So, I was able to bring in photographers like John French and David Bailey, and they began to give newspaper fashion a reputation that it had never had before. Suddenly we were paying big money to these photographers, and you can imagine that got me into a lot of trouble with the accounts department but it made the pages look wonderful!

I was just thirtyish, which in those days was still very young for someone in such a position. I loved putting all the 'Swinging London' stories like kinky boots and hot pants in the newspaper. However, Cecil King, the chairman, who behaved like an emperor, was not similarly charmed. He was about nine feet tall and I remember I met him on the back stairs one day and he stopped me and said, 'When are you going to stop putting these ridiculous clothes in our newspaper?' and I said, 'Well, when they stop being news, Mr King' and he said, 'I don't like them! I would like you to stop putting them in.' And I said, 'What will you do to me if I don't stop putting them in?' and he said, 'I will have you fired.' Oh dear! Anyway I went downstairs and repeated it to Hugh and he said just carry on, carry on, carry on.

And it was fun. It was all such great fun!

# Felicity Green

'LOLLY'

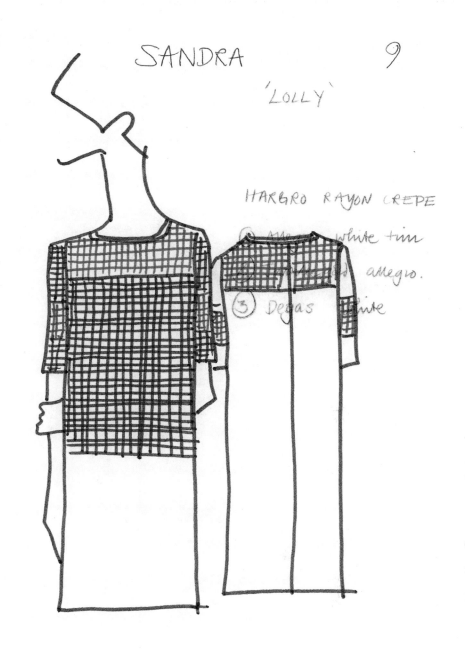

HARGRO RAYON CREPE

① _____ white trim
② _____ allegro.
③ Degas _____

Sketch of rayon crêpe dress, 1965.

NOT GINGHAM

2 colour Rayon Crepe

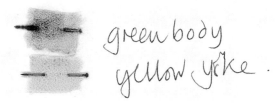

green body
yellow yoke.

Tartan 'mini-suit', c.1966,
*James Wedge.*

**Opposite page:**
The ubiquitous Union
Jack becomes a backdrop for
a miniskirt suit, c.1967.

**I first met Marion and Sally** through Marit [Lieberson, née Allen]. That must have been 1966. For a while I lived at Marit's flat in Redcliffe Square, above where Marion and Geoffrey Kirkland lived. We were pretty friendly with them and we'd meet up at least once a week socially, so I was aware of their work and would go to their shop in Ganton Street. Marit being so involved with Sally and Marion, I became really involved with Geoffrey, who was then the partner of Ridley Scott. They had a design firm together and made furniture. They did lots of things for my first apartment with Marit in Chelsea.

I thought Sally and Marion were wonderful, vital and exciting girls and so much a part of what was happening in London at that time. And they were very open and generous and giving as people, together and individually. They were each totally different in their personalities, they were so different yet they worked so well together, but I didn't really think of them as business partners, they were more like two great friends.

At the time I was working as an agent, principally for actor Peter Sellers and a few other American and European actors and directors in the film industry. There was a whole group of people who would hang out – Sally and Marion and Geoffrey, Sandy Jones and Chester Jones, Ian La Frenais, John Jesse. The sense of London in the mid-sixties was this tremendous coming together of all sorts of creative people. Everyone seemed to mix, rather than being segmented in their various professions. There was a complete breaking down of barriers that people were actually doing consciously. That's what I loved about living in London. If I had been in America I would have mixed with exciting people but they would have all been in the film industry.

The thing that I liked about the Foale and Tuffin boutique is that it had its own style, and it felt like the kind of place that you could go by anytime and just hang out. It was one of the points of social interaction in London; part of a network of places that included Alice Pollock's in Chelsea, Hung On You, Granny Takes a Trip. We used to love going to the Picasso restaurant on the Kings Road, probably the only place still there from that era, and Alvaro's, and the Chelsea Potter. There were lots of places.

Sally and Marion's clothes were fashionable but practical. The big difference at the time was that it was not just about the dress but the look, and the look was very reflective of Marion and Sally. At that time style was a way of life, and fashion was not just about making things to be photographed. It was a moment - everything in fashion at that time was a repudiation of formalized French and Italian designers. The flat shoes, the tights – everything was about function and not just decorative. It liberated women from the trap of fashion. I thought it was incredibly modern and cutting edge. That's how it felt.

I would get my clothes from anywhere I could. Doug Hayward of Fulham. Major Hayward made some great stuff. I met him through Peter Sellers who he made things for and Sean Connery. And I'd go to Savile Row. Huntsman, things like that. A real mix. Completely.

Marion and Sally were so much a part of that 1960s spirit of optimism. They did embody it as people as well as designers. My enduring memory of Sally and Marion's clothes is the miniskirt. Nice. I can remember that instantly.

# Sandy Lieberson

Tartan miniskirt suit, c.1966
*James Wedge.*

**First became aware of Foale and Tuffin** whilst I was at Chiswick Polytechnic studying dress manufacture and design. I saw an article in a fashion magazine, *Vogue* I think, and when in my last year at college I applied to several designers for work, they replied, thinking I had answered an advert in the local jobcentre. I was employed as a sample machinist. I was eighteen years old, had just left college, was young, naive, excited and working in Carnaby Street in 1965! It was quite overwhelming. I was nervous about my first job and my ability. I probably kept quiet and my head down to begin with.

I soon realised Marion and Sally were not like ordinary bosses. There was lots of laughing and people dropping in. I once made a cup of tea for George Harrison and Pattie Boyd when Jenny brought them by. Imagine how that was! Cups of tea, 'biccies' and cigarette smoking; it became like a group of friends working together. The work atmosphere was not as serious as maybe it should have been but somehow it all got done on time.

In the early days I lived outside London near Heathrow and travelled to the West End everyday on the Piccadilly Line, but was soon drawn into living in London to enjoy the social life. We all used to party together. Marion had

a flat in Redcliffe Square and we spent many an hour having drinks on the balcony.

The first workroom I was in was on the corner of Carnaby Street and Ganton Street above Take Six men's shop. They were all very old buildings, creaky wooden stairs and a bit musty-smelling. The room on to Ganton Street was the workroom – two machines and a cutting table; the one on to Carnaby Street was Marion and Sally's design room. It had mirrors and clothes rails and the black leather Chesterfield sofa that seemed to travel from place to place. I wonder what happened to it? When I first arrived, there was another machinist, an older lady called Rose Gray (lovely name) and a bubbly little Greek girl who was the pattern cutter. She was newly married and used to talk about her sex life all the time. I don't remember these two people for very long so I guess they left early on.

The shop was across Carnaby Street in Marlborough Court, opposite The Button Queen and a red telephone box. It wasn't very big and always seemed fun to be in. I remember once the shop was painted all over to resemble blue marble. A technique done using a feather. In the shop was the manager Acushla, Diana and later Jilly. Above the shop was the office where several girls worked during the first years. Along with

all the fashionable clothes shops in Carnaby Street there was a dry-cleaners, and haberdashery shops selling zips, buttons, cottons, etc as the area was predominately tailoring and rag trade. Many of the rooms above shops were tailoring businesses, the like of which are not seen these days. Creaky old winding stairs and shared toilets. Men working in small cramped rooms on wooden benches and using heavy irons.

Later, the workrooms, showroom and office moved across Carnaby Street to the other end of Ganton Street. Cranks vegetarian restaurant and shop was just to the left, Marshall Street Baths was in the next road, and on the corner was Robin's Cafe – great for a Spanish omelette and an apple and raspberry pie with custard!

There were three floors – office and showroom on the first, workroom and kitchen on the second and Marion and Sally's room and the stockroom on the third. The office was at the back of the first floor where Janice and Monica worked, and the showroom was at the front with the black sofa. I was on the second floor with the two sewing machines and a cutting table. Sometimes the samples would come down to me already cut and sometimes I would cut them myself. Sally used to design the softer things such as dresses, skirts and

# Jane Best

shirts. Lots of Liberty prints on both wool and cotton. Marion designed the more tailored garments, jackets, trouser suits and coats. These were mostly sampled at the tailoring factory, but firstly everything was 'toiled' (a tryout shape in calico). Being tallish and a size eight, these were usually tried on me. I also used to model the garments for the buyers when Jenny Boyd was no longer there. My brother Richard often photographed me in the outfits. I remember a silk star suit was an early Zandra Rhodes print.

I guess I used to mostly wear Foale and Tuffin clothes. One of my favourites was a trouser suit called 'Duke'. There was also a coat and a mackintosh along the same lines. Sally used tartan fabric one season for her designs and that was great fun, and there were printed kaftans in both wool and cotton. Another jacket was made of printed velvet with a Victorian influence. It was called 'Mrs Paddy Rabbit', after a garment Sally and her husband Richard had come across. That was another thing – all the garments had names, which Marion still does with her knitwear.

It was great fun being in Carnaby Street at that time. Everybody was happy, smiling and having fun. What more could you want in a work environment? Marion and I used to go for a drink (white wine it was then) after work

in the White Horse pub at the end of Marlborough Court in Newburgh Street and met some interesting people.

Being at F&T it was like a family. We used to talk about our ups and downs, laugh with each other and care for each other. Sally had a dog called Ben, a little Yorkshire terrier, and I fell in love with him so on my twenty-first birthday I got my mum and dad to buy me one. She was called Lucy and also used to come to work. I think I was living in Westbourne Grove at the time and used to take her on the bus.

I guess when the business finished it was just a natural progression. Everybody had met partners by then, some already had moved on. I left in 1971 to go off with my fella to be self-sufficient somewhere in Wales, so for me it had already finished.

I suppose it was a chapter that actually shaped my later life. I remained firm friends with Marion, our respective husbands Christopher and Tony were friends, and although I lived in Wales for some time I still came back to sample and make garments for the shop Marion had in Hinde Street, W1. In the late 1970s we even lived with them in their beautiful thatched farmhouse in Warwickshire. When I decided to move from Wales it was to go somewhere I had friends, and here I am still working with Marion after forty years.

I still see Sally and her family when we get together for reunions and dos, and still keep in touch with other people who worked there.

My memories are of a fun time and good friends made.

Foale and Tuffin Christmas
card, c.1967.

**Opposite page:**
Jane Best models jersey dress,
1967, *Rick Best*.

James Wedge, 1964.

**Opposite page:**
The Foale and Tuffin team, back
row left to right: Marion Foale, Jane
Best, Jean McIntyre. Front row left to
right: Janice Entwhistle, Sally Tuffin,
Acushla Hicks, 1967, *James Wedge*.

**The first Foale and Tuffin dress I saw** was in Woollands 21 Shop, but the first dress I bought was black at the bottom, white at the top, with a check in the middle; or was it white at the bottom? Anyway, it was A-line and made from three different fabrics. To me it was just a miracle. I also had a fabulous ecru lace suit with a wavy front. I remember having that.

I had a miraculous career. I was working for the 'Young Fashion' editor at the *Sunday Times* and she was taken ill and they said, 'You do the job until we find a replacement' and they never did, so I had my own pages. It was very Judy Garland. I was working with the amazing Ernestine Carter. I was her assistant at the beginning, then I had my own pages. We had to tell her to go and see the young designers and their collections and then she became a huge supporter. It was about 1961-1962, so Marion and Sally were starting out just as I was starting my fabulous job.

The thing about the 1950s is that most of us made our own clothes because we couldn't find the things we wanted in the shops. There were Mary Quant's clothes but they seemed expensive. So it was all Simplicity patterns and sewing machines.

Walking into the Foale and Tuffin shop was like walking into your dream, all the stuff you wanted, the kind of stuff you would have made for yourself if they hadn't invented it first! We were the same age and they were designing the kind of clothes you couldn't find and struggled to make yourself. They were just the right ideas, the right people at the right time.

There was something wonderfully homey and amateurish about the early 1960s. Everyone struggling to get their ideas across, not having the financial support but then getting terrific support from the public when they saw what you were doing. Foale and Tuffin were a bit 'home-madey', but not in a bad way. Sally and Marion were designing the clothes, sewing the clothes – it was all so immediate. I think I bought things from every collection.

I loved wearing everything they did and I loved them. They were like close friends. Now the industry is such a huge commercial thing, it's so colossal that you are not likely to get to be friends with the designer, but back then the editors and designers all knew each other. We were all really good friends, like some glorious, amateur whirlpool of creativity.

I still have two long Foale and Tuffin dresses. They are made from seersucker with a round neck, short frilly sleeves, like a tent dress. One is printed with red with white spots alternating with bands of blue and white spots. The other is the same but yellow and orange. Years and years ago I cut it short then regretted it and Sally sent me some fabric but I never got round to stitching it back together.

Those two long dresses – I had fallen in love with this man who had gone to live in Nepal and I bought the dresses with this idea that I could wear them in the balmy evenings, relaxing with a drink. We ended up living in a hut in the jungle, but they kept the mosquitoes off my legs. I married the man and gave up fashion to become a writer.

# Brigid Keenan

**Below left:**
Wrap silk jersey fringed dress,
1967, *James Wedge*.

**Below right:**
Wrap dress with military pocket,
1967, *James Wedge*.

161

Janet Street Porter (right) and Fanny
Ward (left) in floral designs, 1971.

**It was around 1965 that I was first aware of** Foale and Tuffin, when I started studying architecture in London. My college was in Bloomsbury and we used to hang out in Soho and around Carnaby Street a lot, and their shop was in Ganton Street.

It was a brilliant time. Mary Quant was an important designer, as was Gerald McCann, who also has been forgotten about, and John Bates. Too much has been made of minis and hemlines. Foale and Tuffin did clean-cut feminine clothes but they weren't interested in doing cheap stuff, the fabrics were always good. The clothes seemed quite hip and easy to wear, unlike a lot of clothes of the time.

I designed posters and made clothes for another boutique on Carnaby Street called Palisades while I was a student. There was this feeling you could do anything. We got parts in films about 'Swinging London' like *Blow-Up*, we were out every night, going to exhibition openings, fashion shows and music events. A bit like now really. I met Sally later through mutual friends. I would have found it a bit intimidating to meet them when I was a student.

Setting up their business straight from art school, selling their designs in America, wearing their own designs to promote their label – they were trailblazers for a new generation, but I did find their stuff quite expensive. I bought their clothes from about 1971, when I was deputy fashion editor of the *Evening Standard*, and I had big white plastic glasses and quite a severe haircut.

I had a bright red tartan smock dress that I wore with emerald green knee-high suede boots from the Chelsea Cobbler; they had long ribbons that criss-crossed around my legs and looked great with the dress. I wore the dress to a sheep-shearing ball in Northumberland, and got so drunk I fell in a ditch after dancing the 'Gay Gordons' for hours. I was found with my legs, still in the green boots, sticking up in the air. I also had a Liberty print blue fine cotton jumpsuit and there's a picture of me wearing it with Fanny, who was married to Christopher Ward. She's in a Foale and Tuffin dress in the same fabric. We also both had Foale and Tuffin tartan frocks. The picture was taken either walking along the coast in Northumberland, or outside St-Tropez, around 1971. I can't remember exactly where, but we went on holiday together a lot.

# Janet Street Porter

**I taught Sally and Marion at the RCA** when I was working as a freelance teacher. I was also drawing at that time. I remember taking them to the V.&A. to show them clothes from the 1920s and 1930s and they weren't in the least bit interested in them, but then years later I saw them in the museum looking at the very same things for inspiration, so I knew that my force-feeding them those things from the past had worked.

What a lot of people think of as the traditional Liberty prints that they used were actually new prints that I created based on the archive patterns. I worked as a consultant designer for Liberty and that was my style. I was very interested in William Morris and I used art deco and jazz age inspiration, and there was a print called 'Islamic', in my third collection, which pre-empted all that interest in the East that became such a big inspiration for people like Thea Porter.

I never collaborated directly with Foale and Tuffin; they would be shown my collection of textile prints. I suppose it was just that what I did they happened to like and use. My studio was at Merton Abbey, the original William Morris printing works that became the Liberty Printing Mills. That's where all the printing was done, but the girls never came there. They were always shown the collection by an agent. Of course every now and then I used to think, as I was working on a print, 'Oh, that would be a good one for Sally and Marion' and I might draw their attention to it. In the same way that I would think, 'that's one for Saint Laurent.' I used to show Saint Laurent the collection personally in Paris. That was very exciting.

For the Grace Coddington *Vogue* shoot I actually told them what sort of garment I wanted, that I wanted them to add a long ribbon sash, because I directed that photo shoot working with photographer Barry Lategan. When we worked together on shoots he always said he didn't ever need to change anything because he said I had such a great eye for detail. I did all the furniture for that session too – the big cubes, the chaise longue and the cushions with the tassels. It was all very 'Russian Ballet'. And I worked with Barney Wan [art director of *Vogue*] on the layout. The background scene was actually inspired by the *Gazette du Bon Ton*.

I always hugely admired their designs. The outstanding thing throughout was the simplicity of the shapes of their clothes that embodied that little 'dolly bird' image. I think that was probably most influenced by Mary Quant. I lived around the corner from Bazaar so I used to look in all the time to see what she was doing. I used to go to the Foale and Tuffin boutique too. It was in a little side street off Carnaby Street. A little Georgian house, very modest and slightly amateurish in a way. It was just around the corner from Liberty so it was all very handy.

They were definitely trailblazers because what they were doing, setting up on their own, two young girls, hadn't been done before. Nothing like that existed. It's not like now when young designers get grants and sponsorship and help with their business; they just did it themselves.

But I do believe that they couldn't have done it without the pop scene. I think the music scene was immensely important, probably more important than the fashion. Like Ossie [Clark], he was in the right place with the right people like the Rolling Stones.

Sally and Marion were both very much the right style, they had that total 'dolly bird' image, and I suppose if you present the same image that you are selling to your customers then it makes it more real, makes it seem more valid. From the beginning at the RCA they always stood out, because there wasn't another pair like them. There were other students who stood out but the two of them were rather like they were glued together.

# Bernard Nevill

**Sure I photographed their clothes for 'Vogue'.**
They were cute clothes. I remember doing a shoot where we had everything made up in Bernard Nevill prints. Maybe we asked them to make us up something or maybe it was their thing at the time. I did model myself in a couple of the shoots, maybe if it was relevant. Probably Barry [Lategan, the photographer] said, 'We'll put you in it, your hair looks twenties.'

Foale and Tuffin were certainly very girlie. I guess it was that 'Youthquake' time. Their clothes weren't for women; women went to Yves Saint Laurent. But in ready-to-wear everyone was designing for young people, and Foale and Tuffin were very much part of that. There was a whole bunch of them that worked with a very British sensibility. They stayed in Britain, used British fabrics and British manufacturers. It was great for Britain because it promoted all things British.

At that time you bought a dress, wore it to the Ad Lib and then threw it away the next day. I'm very happy that I lived through that period. It was all evolving incredibly quickly. The shift from the 1950s to the '60s was such a big jump. It was all so different, especially in fashion. The designers might turn out hundreds of collections today but they don't really change that much. In the sixties it really evolved from one thing into another and it was so exciting if you were a part of it. But it wasn't so rushed. You'd go on a *Vogue* trip to Africa for two weeks. Now it's two days, and it's not even Africa – it's Miami, and you're trying to make it look like Africa.

At *Vogue* we each had our own little sections and our favourite designers. Marit Allen was very close to Foale and Tuffin. She was totally responsible for putting them on the map, completely.

# Grace Coddington

Jane Birkin models black crêpe
'draughts' trouser suit, 1964, *Bailey/Vogue*
© *The Condé Nast Publications Ltd.*

hat with flower on top, by
yard Mann, £3·10. Floral waist-length
ket with tiered sleeves, £18·50.
ching dungarees, £10·50. Both by
le and Tuffin. White tights, from
olworths, 18p. Sandals, by Sacha, £4·99.
cotton clown top with pompons, £8.
e and-white striped trousers with
ticated cuffs, trimmed with a pompon.

**We met at Walthamstow Art College.** They were students starting their final year. I'd just come out of the navy so Sally and Marion seemed extremely talented and sophisticated. We were all students and did what students do, sharing rent, food and anything else that students share. My first collaboration with them was when I made hats to be worn with their clothes at the Royal College dress show. I was asked by London couturier Ronald Paterson to design hats for his collections. Before I graduated from the Royal College, Liberty's store offered me free workroom space and anything else I needed, in return for supplying them with hats. It grew from there, and then I had my own place just off Carnaby Street where I did my shows and everything. I had shops called Top Gear and Countdown so I started buying clothes from the girls' newly formed company.

A client of mine was Susannah York, and she sold me a second-hand Nikon camera. I was already very good friends with photographers Terence Donovan, Duffy and David Bailey, who all gave me some tips, so I decided to change direction and give it a go. I did a great many editorial shoots using Foale and Tuffin clothes, but the most memorable was a shoot for *Harper's* when I used a watercress farm to represent paddy fields because their clothes had an oriental look about them.

Another shoot was for *19* magazine, photographing clown-like clothes that Foale and Tuffin had produced. I wanted to give them a traditional clown feel without shooting them in an obvious situation like a circus. I decided to shoot them in an old empty warehouse near my studio. I dressed the set by putting old make-up jars on the table and putting pictures torn from Fellini's book on clowns on the walls. I shot in black and white and hand-coloured the printed images. It was all shot in natural light.

There were lots of parties! We were even flown by one host to New York to attend his parties. The 'in' nightclub at the time was the Ad Lib, which was frequented by all the young and beautiful people at that time.

There were so many great Foale and Tuffin designs, but one that I remember that I bought for my shop and was a great seller was a crêpe trouser suit. It had flared trousers and a tunic top that had circular holes cut down the sleeves of the top and the legs of the trousers. It is hard to explain but it was a great design.

It is always sad when talented people split up, and when Sally and Marion split up it was a sad loss for the British fashion industry. It's a good thing that they have remained close friends.

# James Wedge

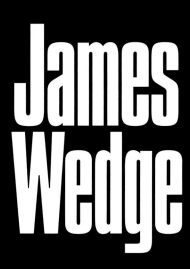

Clown floral frills, 1972, *James Wedge*.

Floral and check quilt Liberty print Varuna wool oriental-style designs, *Harpers and Queen*, September 1971, *James Wedge/The National Magazine Company Ltd.*

TAKE
A
LONG
COOLIE
LOOK

There's a very discernible feeling of Japonaiserie in the air at the moment, and Foale & Tuffin's new autumn collection is part of this – clothes – all in Liberty printed Varuna wool – are oriental peasant-inspired, with quilted mandarin and kimono-style jackets, and straight trousers stopping short above the ankle.

..., SW1. Vicki, Cobham. Japanese nylon socks with divided toe; 72½p, Mitsukiku, 73a Lower Sloane St, SW1 and Brighton. Japanese geta on raised platform; £3.50, Mitsukiku. Big yellow paper umbrella lent by the Display Department at Selfridges, W1. Coolie hat from Japan. ... Very wide quilted midi coat in navy and burnt orange floral print, reversing to navy velvet, with black and cream check edging, £35; worn ... trousers in purple ...

LEFT. Knee-length pinafore
blouse, £11·50, and wide check
length white socks; Ballito, 25p.
RIGHT. Reversible quilted

dress in contrasting bands of check and floral print, £20; worn with chec
trousers, £12·50; Younger Set Department at Harrods; Go to Jericho,
Fenwick, W1. Red canvas mules with wedge heels; £3·60, Biba, 124 High St K
jacket in blue floral print, with short sleeves, £22; worn over ankle-length sl

print, with check quilted hem, £14; Younger Set Department at Harrods; Campus,
Japanese geta sandals in black velvet (we covered them in red braid); £3·50,
and Brighton. Both girls are carrying Japanese parasols in oiled silk, with painted
99 Baker St, W1. Hair and make-up created by Nilo Viyella of New York. Wigs from

Glasgow and Edinburgh. Blo
Mitsukiku, 73a Lower
design; £2·10, Arts &
Wig Wham; 10 Sout

Illustration of oriental floral and quilt collection by May Routh, 1971.
*Photo: Magnus Dennis.*

Ping-Pong.
+
Little Blouse.

Little Blous

←Tea Bags→

Ping-Pong

August-Moon
&
Little
Blouse.

Little Blouse.
Green Tea jacket.
Tea Cosy Skirt

HAPPI JACKET &
CHOPSTICKS

MAX ROUTH.

**I was married to Adrian Bailey** and we lived in Kensington High Street near the store Biba. Gerry Richards, who was at the RCA studying engraving, was our lodger – he later owned the shop Cornucopia. I was very close with a wonderful girl called Winkie MacPherson, who was also at the RCA, as were Marion and Sally, so I became close to them. I think I saw their diploma show when they graduated from the RCA. Sylvia Ayton was there too, and then they set up on their own.

I was drawing, working as a fashion illustrator. It was just so exciting to draw their clothes when I started working for them. The clothes would come to the house and I would draw them on friends. I remember doing these drawings – the mix of prints and colours, the little flowers and checks, the longer jackets, cream-coloured with black binding, and one, two, three ties and a frill at the bottom.

In the 1960s there was still quite a lot of drawing in magazines, as there was throughout the forties and fifties, but by the 1970s illustration was hardly used at all. It was all photography. It more or less evaporated as a career. Fashion illustration was really drying up so I had to find something to do.

I went to work for Marion and Sally as manageress of their little boutique in Marlborough Court – it was so tiny. It was great fun. I certainly didn't have to get in too early and I had an assistant called Jilly, who was this wonderful girl with curly red hair. She was about seventeen years old and very pretty and seemed to know all the gossip. Most of the time she told me what to do!

I remember the first day I worked there, Jilly had gone out to lunch and a man came in, he was absolutely hideous-looking and he came up to the counter and said to me: 'Women like to dress me up in women's clothes!' I thought, 'Get me out of here!' The minute Jilly walked in he rushed out. They were really exciting times.

I'd have to open up the shop. It was so exciting when people wanted to try things on and buy things. Of course there were days when they'd try things on, drop them on the floor and not buy a thing and you'd be left having to pick them up. Then it was really quite boring.

The atmosphere was quite relaxed in the shop. Someone would say I'm going out to lunch now, nobody clocked in and out. Sally and Marion were just around the corner in Ganton Street so we'd pick up the phone and say we'd need someone to come round and

they did. It was a very friendly easy-going atmosphere.

What was exciting was that it wasn't just famous pop stars' girlfriends who shopped there, but also women would come in who were married to a good-looking cameraman – it was glamorous by connection.

I remember Ernestine Carter came into the shop and I was really proud to serve her. Coral Browne came in too, but I don't think she bought anything, but it was still exciting. Everyone came in.

It was not like Biba where there were lots of people; remember, it was a tiny little shop. People either liked the clothes or they wouldn't be in the shop. They were definitely Sally and Marion type people. The people who came in were very devoted, they'd come in and shop for lots of things at one go and then we wouldn't see them for six months, then they'd come back and do another big shop.

Marion and Sally were designing for people of their generation. Their clothes were mostly under £20; everyone could afford them. I think there was one thing that I lusted after that was about £70 – it was a long waistcoat lined in fake fur fabric.

They were producing so many collections a year, not very big but very personal,

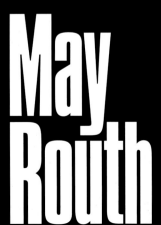

# May Routh

everything interrelated. They were just very intelligent; they understood how people bought things and what people wanted to wear. They wore the things. They looked adorable. You didn't need to see it on a six-foot model. They were quite small and they were designing for that kind of woman – women like themselves.

I remember there was a jacket I fell in love with, it was a very popular style called 'Sweet William'. It had ties in the front with short sleeves and was made from two different Liberty print cottons. Later they made the same jacket in wool. The girls were very clever, they let me think I was doing the buying for the shop, but really they did it. I remember I really didn't like the colour green, I really thought green was ugly and they did this whole green look and to my horror it sold really well.

There were lots of different groups of people around; I was more into the art scene, but there was a great crossover – the arts world, the film world, music. Photographer Brian Duffy was my first boyfriend when I was at St Martin's School of Art. People

It was a great fun time.

Then suddenly it all changed, there was the awful three-day week and the whole thing blew up in our faces. We'd say, 'But we're in "Swinging London", this can't be happening!' It was just weird. Marion and Sally were very smart; maybe they could see that it was the end of that era.

I had been asked by Yvonne Blake to do drawings for the costumes for *Jesus Christ Superstar* and then I ended up assisting her on the film *Three Musketeers*. In 1974 I moved to America.

When they broke up Marion moved to Nuneaton. Sally continued the label – I've still got one of the blouses she did – then she did a mail-order catalogue, and then Marion started knitting. I never thought they would split up, I guess you never think about things like that at the time. So I was pretty devastated when they did. I wasn't sure what was going to happen. It's nice that it was amicable and they stayed friends; they are like family really.

**in the winter of 1961 I left Somerset** to start a new life in London. The atmosphere was exciting because of the awareness of change in the styles of music, art and fashion.

On the grapevine in 1963 I heard that hat designer James Wedge was looking for a model/personal assistant. After the interview he said I had the job, but he needed the opinion/approval of two of his friends. We walked around the corner to Marlborough Court, up to the first floor workroom where I was introduced to Marion Foale and Sally Tuffin. I knew their names and label but had never ventured into wearing their avant-garde clothes. It was exciting to feel close to the heart of this new revolution.

During the four years I worked with James Wedge our paths often crossed, and a friendship with Sally and Marion developed. During this time Foale and Tuffin became more and more successful and in 1968, after returning from travelling in Europe, I ran into Sally in Berwick Street Market in Soho. She asked if I wanted a job, as they needed a production manager. I accepted, and the following four years working with Foale and Tuffin was a challenge, and fun.

By now, they were at the peak of their success, and established as a design house. Orders were flooding in from America, Italy, Scandinavia, as well as the home market. My particular role was to translate these garment orders into fabric lengths, colourways, quantities to quilt, and so forth, to ensure we had enough cloth to fulfil the orders; then to get the clothes made at the factory, and delivered on time. Thanks to an efficient factory and a fantastic local van driver, we usually got the clothes for the London boutiques delivered on time. Shipping the overseas orders was always a tedious job.

The Foale and Tuffin studio/showroom in Ganton Street was a pleasant place to work because, as well as their huge talent and success, there was a selfless modesty with both Sally and Marion, and they had a genuine grateful respect for each of their staff. For example, every design was given a name and we were all invited to take part in the naming process. So, a heavy wool overcoat was called 'Napoleon'; a kaftan, 'Luxor'. An ankle-length Liberty Veruna wool tiered dress with wide tiered sleeves was 'Hurdy Gurdy'. Every piece had its own identity.

We were an all women company. There were six to eight of us including Sally, Marion, Marylyn the house model, Jane the sample machinist, Janice the accountant, and Jilly and Sally who ran the boutique. Our days were spent working hard but we always had a break for a shared lunch bought at Cranks, across the road. We enjoyed sitting on the floor around the glass showroom table with our communal lunch, sharing ideas, often joined by Marit Allen, their friend from *Vogue*, or maybe John Swinfield, the sales manager for Liberty Prints, or Jo Bergman, an American customer/friend. The showroom was always a sociable place, with fashion journalists, special personal customers who could not find the right size for them in the Foale and Tuffin boutique in Marlborough Court, photographers and set designers calling in to view the collections and borrow samples for publicity. It was always buzzing.

As I saw it, Marion was the soft-edged tailor and Sally the soft-edged dress designer. They designed separately but shared ideas, and above all had a close understanding of one another. There was a time when they even physically resembled one another. Have you seen the black and white photo?

Among my favourite outfits was the three-piece wool jersey suit with long slim jacket, slim trousers and skirt, a printed cotton velvet jacket, above the knee but below the thigh, slim-fitting and tight-sleeved ('Paddy Rabbit'); a reversible quilted Liberty Tana lawn short sleeved jacket ('Sweet Pea') with ties at the front and subtle long peplum, best worn over a Liberty print long-sleeved blouse, and perhaps a pair of quilted Tana lawn hot pants!

The trouser suit was a favourite with most of us there but no one appeared to embrace the idea of liberation or rebellion. Our behaviour did not change. It felt like a natural progression. Probably, with the softness of the fabrics and gentleness of the design, one still felt and looked feminine. Although I imagine Marion and Sally felt liberated by their achievement and success.

It was sad and disturbing when Foale and Tuffin split in the 1970s, but we all understood. Lives and times were changing direction, with marriage and families ahead. Nothing could stay the same forever. I stayed on with Sally Tuffin until 1972 when our daughter was born and my husband and I moved to Dorset. Later, in 1975, when Sally, Richard and their young family moved to Somerset, we worked together for a few years creating Tuppence Coloured, a mail-order company selling children's clothes kits which Sally designed.

They were happy days with Foale and Tuffin, and what a fortunate experience. It felt like the right place at the right time. However, today, most us of us are still in touch and good friends, so the story continues.

# Monica Renaudo

The Foale and Tuffin team outside the shop in Marlborough Court, left to right: Jilly McCormack, Marylyn Larkin, Sally Fleetwood, Sally Tuffin, Marion Foale, Jane Best, Janice Entwhistle, Monica Renaudo, c.1968, *James Wedge*.

**We opened the store in March 1970** at 27 South Molton Street, on one floor only. There was already a shop here called Browns, owned by Sir William Piggott-Brown, which Mr Burstein bought, and we changed it. My aim was to be focused and individual, appealing to the fashion conscious girl. We were definitely keen to support British designers, they were all doing their own thing and everything was very individual.

Foale and Tuffin were producing quite romantic, ethnic-inspired looks at the time – I guess fashion was looking more outwardly at new worlds and alternatives to Western culture and values. They were the Marni of their day, and different from the run-of-the-mill. They were always appealing, fresh and young. But they had quality: they were on another level compared with many of the other young designers at that time.

Moving from the 'Swinging Sixties' into the escapist seventies, the British designers set the mood: Foale and Tuffin, Mary Quant, Ossie Clark, Biba, Bill Gibb – young designers who set the mood for the times. Carnaby Street was buzzing – there were so many designers, and yet Foale & Tuffin were unique. The only designers similar I can think of would be Pablo & Delia.

Part of Foale and Tuffin's success was that they were designing for young women just like themselves. They had a point of view of their own, and that was very important. My lasting memories of the era? Romantic, young at heart, whimsical designers. It was such an exciting era, which one only appreciates when it has gone.

# Joan Burstein

*Daily Mirror* honours the world
of fashion, the Dorchester, 1970.

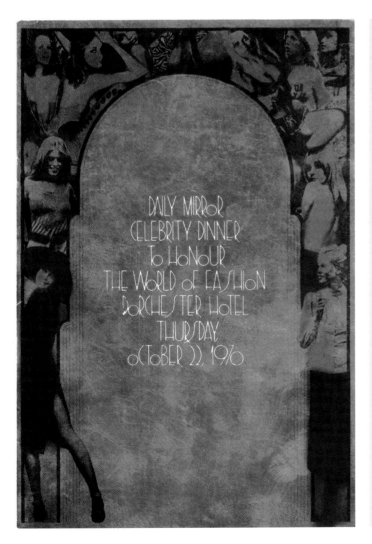

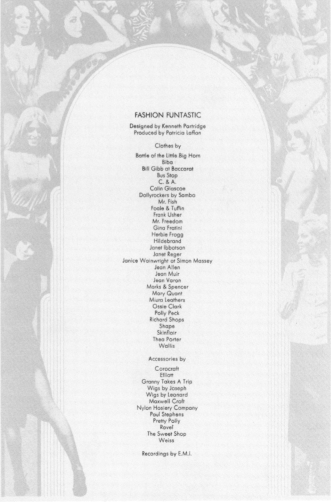

FASHION FUNTASTIC

Designed by Kenneth Partridge
Produced by Patricia Laffan

Clothes by

Battle of the Little Big Horn
Biba
Bill Gibb at Baccarat
Bus Stop
C. & A.
Colin Glascoe
Dollyrockers by Samba
Mr. Fish
Foale & Tuffin
Frank Usher
Mr. Freedom
Gina Fratini
Herbie Frogg
Hildebrand
Janet Ibbotson
Janet Reger
Janice Wainwright at Simon Massey
Jean Allen
Jean Muir
Jean Varon
Marks & Spencer
Mary Quant
Miura Leathers
Ossie Clark
Polly Peck
Richard Shops
Shape
Skinflair
Thea Porter
Wallis

Accessories by

Coracraft
Elliott
Granny Takes A Trip
Wigs by Joseph
Wigs by Leonard
Maxwell Croft
Nylon Hosiery Company
Paul Stephens
Pretty Polly
Ravel
The Sweet Shop
Weiss

Recordings by E.M.I.

Mixed Liberty floral print full-
length smock dresses, 1971, *David
Hamilton/Vogue* © *The Condé Nast
Publications Ltd.*

**Foale and Tuffin reflected exactly** how it was from the 1960s through to the mid-1970s. They very much reflected young girls at that time, what they wanted to wear, who they wanted to be. They were the same as the young girls.

They started with simple little frocks, things we were all wearing; dresses that stood out and had a shape. Very simple, cutaway dresses. The Audrey Hepburn thing. At that time it was all about the word 'dolly'. We even wore little bar strap shoes in bright colours! Fashion had become something that wasn't what your parents had worn, ever. It was far more creative and much faster. It was all about creativity and being fast. The Foale and Tuffin boutique in Marlborough Court was tiny. The street was almost Dickensian. But being in that area was terribly important, whether it was in Carnaby Street, Kingly Street, Newburgh Street or the rest.

From 1965-69 I was on Rave magazine and worked at Radio 1. I remember a lot of raving in discotheques but there's a lot I don't remember. I do remember crochet dresses and hot pants and miniskirts, but the mini in those days was right down to the knees. It's funny to think it caused such a horror for Jean Shrimpton in Australia at Gold Cup Day.

What happened next was a total explosion! Think about The Beatles – they went from that clean-cut look to the hippy thing, so fashion went pretty and 'floaty' and mystical. It was all very pretty and romantic with lots of frills and flowers. Lots of Victoriana references too. Suddenly people had had enough of the rigid simplicity, and so straight after all those sculpted Jackie Kennedy and Audrey Hepburn looks they wanted something more interesting. Liberty prints were interesting; we even did up our homes in them too. I remember a friend said to me, 'Your hat looks wonderful because it's dressed like you are!' I remember Marion and Sally did fabulous shirts as well and we were all wearing their boot-leg trousers and nipped in jackets.

Fashion moved so quickly from the sixties to the seventies. Looking back you think, 'Woaoww! Where did that come from?' Fashion was changing so fast, changing completely from one turn of the page to the next.

Sally and Marion were very opinionated. They weren't wobbly little girls. It was an immensely strong time for women. From 1969 I was on the *Daily Mail* assisting Jean Rook, and I remember being sent by David English, my editor on the *Daily Mail*, to infiltrate a cell of feminists in Camden. We fought hard for acceptance – money, position and an equal role in society – but you weren't ever going to get a London girl to give up her sexuality. The American feminists were much more radicalized – they hated our Page Three girls. In 1971 I joined the *Daily Mirror* as assistant to Felicity Green. I became fashion editor at the *Mirror* in 1974.

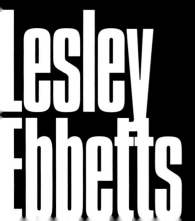

# Lesley Ebbetts

Opposite page:
Turquoise silk jersey pyjama suit, 1969

**I first became aware of Foale and Tuffin** when I bought a Liberty print kaftan to wear to the Rolling Stones concert in Hyde Park in 1969. I bought it from a shop in Kensington High Street. It was loose and light and perfect for that hot summer day. I felt at home in it instantly. That was rare for me. Unlike most of the 'dolly birds' of the sixties, who were tall, thin and flat-chested, with long flowing hair, I was short, round and busty with a curly mop of hair. I tended to wear dresses down to the ground, which was my only real style. So, a dress that fit, (not unimportant) and was bright and fun, was fantastic. I needed more of them.

I'm not exactly sure how I found my way to their shop off Carnaby Street, but I remember trying on a dress there and getting stuck. I was afraid to try and take it off for fear of ripping it. So I just shouted for help and Sally came round from the workshop and got me out of it. She had a good giggle, and then figured out how to alter it so it would fit me.

I was working for the Rolling Stones at the time. I was Mick's personal assistant and ran the office in London. My life was chaotic, exactly like the lives of all my friends. London was a village and it seemed that everyone you knew was connected to everyone else by only a few degrees of separation. For example, I didn't realize at the time that Sally and Marion were close friends of Marit Allen, who worked for *Vogue* and was married to Sandy Lieberson, Mick's movie agent and producer. I was planning to go on tour with the Stones and I needed to figure out clothes so I wouldn't have to think about them. Marit immediately told me to see Sally and Marion.

I went to the Foale and Tuffin workshop round the corner from Cranks health-food restaurant – and it was like entering Ali Baba's cave. We gathered in the small office and had tea and buns from Cranks. I got to look at the collection – fabulous Liberty prints in glorious combinations. This was the first of many times that I got to select a whole wardrobe. The girls who worked there joined us and laughed a lot as I tried to squeeze into the model sizes – not unlike the first time I'd gone to the F&T shop. I picked the dresses and the fabrics and the jackets and the coats, and they would make them work for me. I was in heaven.

The first collection I bought was the Chinese quilted one. I still have most of it in a suitcase. It is probably my favourite. It toured Europe. It toured America. It moved with me to New York. It is timeless.

Sally and Marion's clothes are magical – they make the wearer feel original, comfortable, witty and happy. I've never been as much myself as in their clothes. I wore them on every occasion – they went all over the world with me. I was so accustomed to wearing them that I was absolutely devastated when they closed their doors. I truly didn't know who I was. How could I find another external expression of my self, my imagination? I don't think I ever have.

# Jo Bergman

# how you should look

JIM LEE (left) chose Quorum
black and yellow suit,
£14 8s. 6d. STEVE HIETT
(right) chose red floaty dress
and trousers by Foale & Tuffin:
dress, 12½ gns., trousers, 7 gns.
from 113 Kings Road,
London, S.W.3.

Liberty silk print dress and trousers
featuring print by Bernard Nevill,
*Petticoat* magazine, c.1969, *Steve Hiett*.

Sally in matelot stripe top, 1964.

Long creamy cotton dress
with full sleeves, a
drawstring neckline and
a matching tie belt, by
Foale and Tuffin, £12 10s.
Blue cotton paisley
full long skirt has an
elasticised waistline,
£9 10s. Matching blouse
has short sleeves, and
elasticised waist and
neckline, £6 10s. Both
by Foale and Tuffin.
Embroidered woollen belt
worn round head, by Rosie
Nice in Kensington
Market, 42s. Belt, from
Susan Locke, £2.

**I was a Foale & Tuffin shopper.** They were part of the Carnaby Street thing when it used to be a destination. They were before Biba. They used to have this lovely little shop just off Carnaby Street. I don't know how Foale & Tuffin got on to the grapevine, and why we all wanted a part of it, maybe it was because all the people like Pattie Boyd would be wearing it and we all wanted to look like her and Twiggy too; Cathy McGowan as well. I was wondering how did we know about these things at that time, but I guess it was the same as now, basically it was the celebrities of the day who were wearing it, and then they were featured in the newspapers. There was that great journalist Felicity Green on the *Daily Mirror*.

You just had to go there every week to get something. All of us were on our little salaries so you'd save your money up. It wasn't quite as inexpensive as Biba was but it was just the place. It was all about the mini and then they did all this great coloured towelling stuff and they were using zips a lot. I just remember this dress that I had to have. Britain was so swinging then. The clothes were so cool. Amazing.

It was exactly when I started my career in the fashion business and everyone was running around in a version of their little dresses and the Vidal Sassoon haircut, and then it was the hippy thing, the Woodstock thing, and the Stones had happened. When I started at *Nova* the mini was just about ending and the maxi was starting. There was that huge shift and the whole thing changed and we got into floral patterns, and that was when Bill Gibb was emerging, but Bill was terribly expensive and at *Nova*, where we were like the first street magazine, we wanted to show an alternative to the top designers.

I remember doing a peasant story for *Nova*. That was lovely. April 1971. I think the hippy thing had happened. That was a huge movement, and we grew our hair, and the ethnic scene then led to Kenzo. Oh gosh, wasn't it gorgeous, that whole peasant thing. There was Laura Ashley too.

It was a time of big change. People began to challenge America. It was the beginning of the gradual change of power and, in fashion, of the influence of the president's wife or the Queen or the establishment. That was when 'street fashion', which hadn't been coined as a phrase yet, really began to have a big influence, and then Laura Ashley of course came out at that time with those floral prints – very nostalgic, shepherdesses, almost historical. It was the beginning of the huge influence of the textiles too.

Then glamour kicked in and took over from the hippy. It's fascinating looking at it now, how the pendulum just goes backwards and forwards. Except now it's so fast.

I've still got one of those Foale & Tuffin dresses; it's all different Liberty prints because they used to work a lot with Liberty prints. I loved all the colour. It was an ethnic look because the hippies took us to Morocco.

I wonder if this was the same time that Kenzo had got to Paris? That was a huge shift in pattern on pattern, print on print, and they did these really romantic dresses with big sleeves. That was when we wanted to look really girlie. And we wore their gorgeous, lovely blouses. And then they did that 'clown look'. I was so much a Foale & Tuffin girl, because of course everyone went to Ossie, but Ossie you just couldn't afford.

I think it's a shame that they didn't survive the fashion thing as a design team because they were obviously very tuned into what was going on. So I'm sure they could still be doing it. Their dresses could be in magazines now.

# Caroline Baker

**Previous spread:**
Cotton voile spot and check
Gypsy dress, c.1971, *John Bishop/
IPC Magazines*.

Floral and quilt designs get the
peasant treatment in *Nova*, styled
by Caroline Baker, 1971, *François
Lamy/IPC Magazines* (below left
and right).

*Best Wishes for Christmas and New Year from*

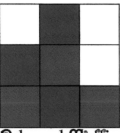

Role and Muffin

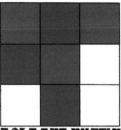

**DOLE AND NUFFIN**

Huffin and Puffin

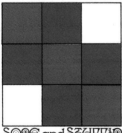

SOLE and STUFFIN

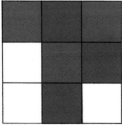

**FOALE AND TUFFIN LTD**

Foale and Tuffin Christmas card, c.1966.

**Foale and Tuffin did little dresses**, something nice to wear to go to a wedding or to lunch. They had that nice little business off Carnaby Street, that was pleasant to go to. They appealed to the fashion press at the time. They weren't as outré as Ossie Clarke, who was my great friend. I was fashion editor of *Nova* at the time.

Mary Quant came first. She was at art school when I was at Goldsmiths doing painting. Mary Quant had the social kudos of [Alexander] Plunkett-Green alongside her. She had a man behind her, and then Archie [McNair], the accountant, came along and he put those two on the map.

Barbara Hulanicki had Fitz [husband Stephen Fitz-Simon] behind her. They were a team as well. Lee Bender of Bus Stop had her husband. Foale and Tuffin were just two girls, and we did like the idea of two girls just getting on with it. Sally and Marion just got on with it. And they never got contaminated by business or money, they just did their own thing. I did like the idea of that.

# Molly Parkin

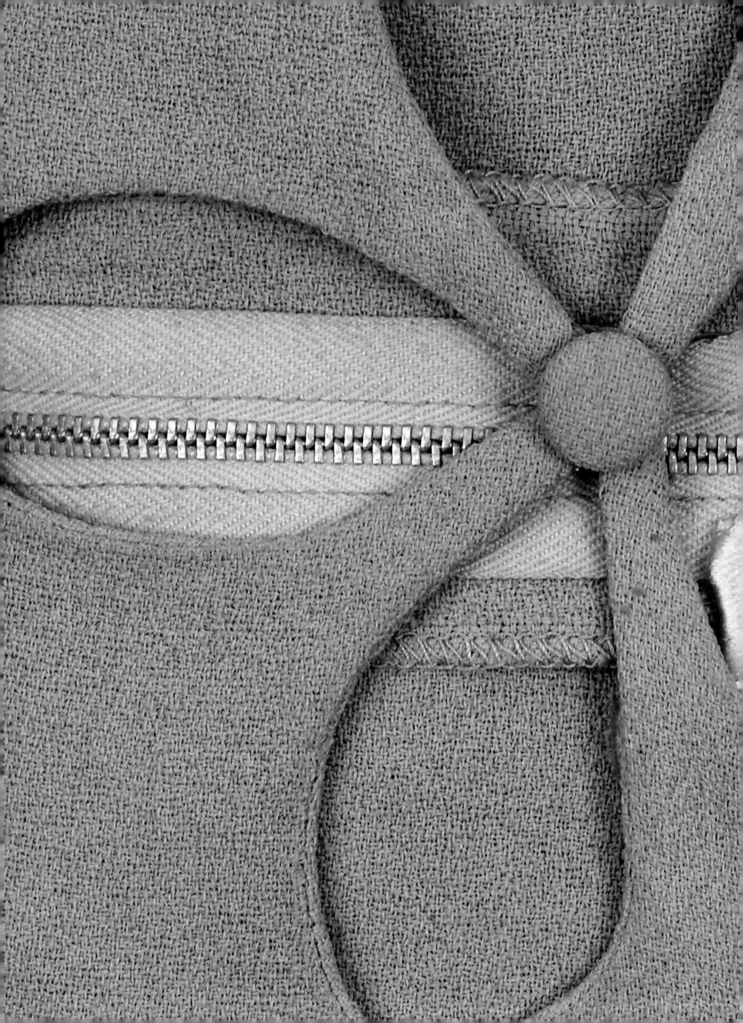

Previous spread:
Pink rayon crêpe daisy blouse
with early Foale and Tuffin label,
c.1963/4 *Photo: Magnus Dennis*.

Below: 'Napoleon' raincoat
designed for Dannimac, c.1966,
*David Hicks*.

Opposite page:
Yellow and shocking pink
towelling shift dress, 1967.

**I went to the Royal College of Art** from 1953-56, so I was no longer there when Sally and Marion attended the fashion school from 1959-61, but they were the golden years in the painting school with people like Ron Kitaj, David Hockney, Peter Phillips, Allen Jones and Derek Boshier. It was an incredible year.

I had befriended Derek Boshier, so through him I met the other students. His girlfriend was Pauline Fordham. I socialised with the painters, and Pauline Boty was studying stained glass at the time. Derek shared a room with Jon Manasseh and Pauline [Boty] and Celia Birtwell had lodgings in the same house. We all lived around West London – Chiswick, Holland Park, Kensington, Notting Hill and Shepherd's Bush. We were part of a group that hung out together, so we would be eating out together in various restaurants. We went to the Hoop and Toy pub in South Kensington. And I met everyone at parties. I was a decade older but we were part of a larger circle of friends.

When I went to the RCA in 1953, that six years made a lot of difference. It was relatively close to the end of the war so it was still quite schooly back then. We certainly used the common room, and on the top floor at 21 Queensgate, opposite the Natural History Museum, there was a music room and they had a music club. On the first floor was a canteen where we'd all have lunch. It was a very social event. And parties took place there too. I remember Janey Ironside and John Minton getting incredibly drunk.

From talking to Sally and Marion I was aware of what they were doing from the beginning. They started their partnership at college. And then their clothes started to be photographed in the magazines. They were quite famous pretty quickly.

That was before Ossie Clark was on the scene. Celia always talked about Ossie. She'd say, "You wait till Ossie gets here. He'll knock the socks off you."

I was always interested in what Sally and Marion were doing and liked the clothes they were designing. That eventually led to commissioning them to make the wedding dress for my first wife Jann Haworth. It was the lace dress with a keyhole. I think we bought other things at the time.

At that time there was a general interest in and a crossing-over of ideas. I always say it was a kind of Renaissance. I think I had some kind of influence on Derek, Peter and maybe even Allen Jones, although I'd never claim such, so that influence probably crossed over to fashion as well. And, of course, there was the music. We were all seeing the same bands – watching The Beatles, and later on The Who, emerge. Ideas passed to and fro.

We'd go to the Foale and Tuffin shop up a tiny alley off Carnaby Street. It was a tiny little shop, with bare, sanded wooden floors that were becoming the fashion then. Very simple and very minimal so it must have seemed slightly out of step with the other shops, and been seen as something avant-garde at the time.

That area had been a fashion place for some time, certainly since the mid-fifties. There was a store called Vince, a menswear shop. Pauline Fordham opened her shop Palisades on the other side of the road, so it was becoming very fashion and hip. I think the fashion designers were probably inspired by what we painters were doing. I remember I gave Pauline my entire collection of Superman comics and she papered a wall and made a mural. And Derek designed her windows.

And then there was Biba. It was the first time that girls could go into Biba and buy relatively inexpensive clothes. There was a definite excitement in the air.

Just like other young women like Pauline Boty and Pauline Fordham, I think Sally and Marion were just speaking up for themselves.

They were finding a place for themselves. Although I wasn't keen on the rampant feminism, women like Germaine Greer, I was certainly sympathetic to the idea of it. I did believe in equality, I thought that we should have women painters. I was sympathetic to the idea.

My career literally started as we turned into 1961, the year Sally and Marion started their label. I was beginning to teach. On Mondays I taught analytical drawing at St Martins with Joe Tilson, on Tuesdays I taught illustration at Harrow and then painting at Walthamstow. I would socialise with the students as I was only two or three years older than them, because I'd started so young. So I would mix with Ian Dury and Peter Greenaway, who were both at Walthamstow. I would probably have been drinking the night before so I often went to teach with a hangover.

Although I left college in 1956, 1961 was the key year for me. I won the junior prize in the Henry Moore competition and Ken Russell made *Pop Goes The Easel*, his first documentary film for the BBC TV Monitor arts series, which introduced the public to Pop Art. I had a show, 'Blake Boty Porter Reeve', at the AIA Gallery in Lisle Street with Pauline and Geoff Reeve and Christine Porter, and then the first *Sunday Times* came out and they did an article on me. It was the start of that phase of my career. And then almost exactly late 1969, I moved to Somerset. The Sixties really defined that bit of my career. I didn't do any drugs but there was a definite Swinging Sixties mood – the music, the liveliness. And at the end of the decade there was a general turning away from it. For some it was disillusionment, for some it was just moving on. People like Dick Smith moved to the West Country, as did Howard Hodgkin and Joe Tilson. The Sixties were over and people were moving on.

It all happened very quickly.

# Peter Blake

# THE ESSENCE OF THE SIXTIES

**Foale and Tuffin conversation three**
Iain R. Webb

**I want to talk about the different projects and collaborations that you were involved with. Tell me about what happened with the men from Dannimac?**

M / (laughs) It was horrendous really. Well, I think you can guess, can't you? All I can remember was the three or four men in grey suits sitting in our showroom.
s / Sitting in our showroom saying, 'Is there a man we can talk to?' And we said, 'No there aren't any men. No men here.' (laughs)
M / You would never have thought they were in the world of making ladies' clothes. They were just grey men.
s / But they were shattered that they couldn't talk to any men, seriously shattered.
M / And it was just us two little young things.

**And had they approached you?**

s / Yes, and we were doing it anyway.
M / We were doing the raincoats.
s / And it was going quite well wasn't it?
M / Yes it was. I don't know whether they saw the coat in *Here We Go Round the Mulberry Bush* [film, 1967], and that's why they got in touch with us. Who wore that? We went up to their factory, don't you remember? It was near Bradford and it was so grey. It was the greyest thing I think I have ever done in my life.
s / It must have been about the time of that film, as one of them was wearing the 'Napoleon' coat.
M / Yes, the first one was a take on the 'Napoleon'.

**Another collaboration was the Sindy doll? Tell me how you got involved when they launched Sindy.**

M / They approached us. I don't know how they found us?
s / I think it was through Vanessa and some marketing thing, and she told them they ought to get some young designers for the project.

**She was certainly the doll with the hippest clothes.**

M / And she wasn't like Barbie because Barbie was far too sexy and sexual for English girls, and Sindy had to be like the girl next door.
s / And we did a collection of clothes for her.
M / When they wanted it, every six months.

**What kind of things did you do?**

M / I remember the ski outfit and the raincoat outfit. The Dannimac outfit!
s / We did versions of what we were doing, so very early on we did little straight tartan skirts and knit tops.

**I think that outfit was called 'Lunch Date'. They all had names?**

M / Yes, they all had names.
s / We never did evening dresses.
M / Well, the nearest to that was the pink dress with a frill at the hem edged in lace. It was like a teenage party dress because it was meant to be a teenage thing, it wasn't meant to be womanly.

**And you made everything to scale.**

M / Oh yes, and we've still got the patterns.

**But you weren't happy with the illustrations on the box.**

M / I didn't like that image at all.
s / We certainly wouldn't have drawn like that. In our drawings we didn't have hair like that, we didn't have eyes like that, we didn't have hands like that.
M / We just didn't do that.
s / And we certainly wouldn't have carried a little wash-bag like the one that goes with the 'Babydoll' nightie.

**Although the doll actually has the look of the sixties 'dolly girl', the illustrations are very fifties, aren't they? Highly stylized and much more couture-like. And very 'done up'.**

M / Yes. We didn't think much to it.

**But it was a good thing to do.**

M / It was. If only we'd have stuck at it! (both laugh) We were stupid.
s / Why did we stop?
M / Well, it was a fiddle to do, and we were then making a lot of stuff anyway.
s / Did we just say no more?
M / Yes. We just said we don't want to do it anymore.
s / Did we?
M / Yes. We must have been mad.
s / I don't think it was a very good earner.
M / It wasn't bad. It was a nice little earner on the side.
s / But I don't think we got any royalties.
M / But if we had stuck with it I think we could have put our foot down.
s / We do have a friend who turned down the marketing of *Star Wars*, so I don't feel so bad.

**We've talked about *Kaleidoscope*, but what about *Two for the Road*, with Audrey Hepburn and Albert Finney?**

M / *Two for the Road*. Lady Rendlesham was the costume person on that and she asked us and Paco Rabanne to make things.

**And obviously Audrey Hepburn was a real Givenchy girl, so that must have seemed a real coup for you?**

M / We did a white suit. I loved it. It was great that we did that.
s / But we never met her.
M / No we didn't, but we had all her sizing, and I can remember delivering it to the Westbury hotel.

**Another person that you collaborated with a lot was James Wedge, who made such wonderful hats.**

M / Yes, he did the white hat that went with the white suit in *Two for the Road*.

**You obviously knew him from the beginning, but was it a decision to get him to do hats to go with your outfits?**

M / He was just the milliner of the time and a really clever person.
S / He just was there.
M / And we were friends
S / And stylists would put him together with our designs. We never commissioned a hat did we? We used to buy his hats to sell in the boutique.
M / Yes we did, and then he opened his boutiques, Top Gear and Countdown, and he stocked loads of our stuff.
S / And one in Bristol.

**So there was a real synergy.**

M / Yes, and we were all working round the same area – Ganton Street and Fouberts Place and around there.

**I have been really blown away by his hats.**

M / He's very clever isn't he? He's multi-talented. He's done so many things.
S / At one stage he was making hats for Liberty and they asked him to do all the windows in Regent Street for Christmas, and he was quite worried but he came up with such brilliant things. I remember thinking how brilliant they were.

**And then the handbags.**

M / Oh, yes, Sally Jess. I've still got a couple of them and so have you. I've got a white leather one.
S / Mine are black and orange patent. And I've got a bracelet from Plush Kicker.

**So how did you get involved with Sally? Was she doing things specifically for you?**

S / Well, John [Jesse] has always lived near us. He had a shop down Kensington Church Street.
M / And they were married at that stage.
S / So we knew them socially.
M / Sally worked in the shop at one point and that's when Mick Fleetwood [her brother] used to come around, and met Jenny Boyd and married her. I don't know why she [Sally] did handbags.
S / I don't know why. John used to do a lot of art deco stuff, and was probably doing his shirts then.
M / Did they not collect a lot of Bakelite type handbags of that period and that might have inspired her?

**And were they commissioned?**

S / We sold them in the shop.
M / I think she just did a range and we chose that one and that one and that one.
S / I remember we used to match them up with things we wore.
M / They were perfect at that time with the clothes and with the white boots.
S / And of course there was a Courrèges influence there.

**Very pop art.**

M / Mondrian.
S / There were lots of white ones, pale blue ones.
M / I've got the white. Well it's my mum's actually (laughs).

**And then much later the 'car-paint' red patent Japanese sandals?**

S / Where did we get those? We all had them didn't we?
M / I didn't.
S / I think it was somewhere in Regent Street that did them, a bit like a clog person. Oh, I know, it was Elliot's of Bond Street. And we wore them like ordinary shoes, which is amazing now because I try them on and they really are a bit dangerous.

**They definitely are an extension of that clog thing.**

M / Yes. We all wore clogs and we all wore the Scholl sandal that came in after that.

**Yeah, my sister had those. She just wore a Norwegian sweater and Dr. Scholl sandals.**

M / Clack, clack, clacking about.
S / And we wore them because we were wearing Japanese type clothes.

**Let's talk labels. I am assuming this dress with the two name-tag labels simply sewn side by side is very early on.**

M / It is. We did it at MacCulloch & Wallis. We hadn't got a lot of money to spend so the cheapest way was to buy their ordinary, brownish cinnamon type coloured ribbon, or whatever colour ribbon it was, and then it was printed on top. It was the cheapest way of doing labels. And then later on, when we could afford to, we went to Cash's.
S / It was all lower case then as well, the font.

**And it was quite a large label.**

M / It was large. There was quite a lot to get on.
S / We had cream ones with red writing and black ones with white writing. And the cream ones went in the paler colours and the dark ones in the darker colours. It was as simple as that. And they even went in small things like shirts.
M / Yes, they were big but I think we wanted them to be big and also there were a lot of words to fit in. You had to get in 'Made in England' on.

**And the graphic was very pop art. A few others have turned up. 'Foale and Tuffin for Daphne Dresses'?**

M / That's a new one on me?

**American maybe?**

s / Paraphernalia?

**And Foale and Tuffin for 'Youthquake'. Was that when you did the 'Youthquake' tour?**

s / Yes.
m / And sometimes they would put a Paraphernalia label in as well.
s / And that was all under the Puritan Fashions Corporation.

**But you'd been to America before that trip hadn't you?**

m / Yes, but just with a suitcase full of stuff and met John Kloss.

**And the 'Youthquake' trip was in 1965. So how did the name get changed round to Tuffin and Foale in America?**

m / It just did.
s / At the beginning Marion said, 'It's got to be Foale and Tuffin because it's alphabetical order.'
m / They just did it, so it was great because we both got a shot at being first.
s / And also they could never get the name right anyway which is why we did that card.
m / 'Huffin and Puffin' and … it was a Christmas card wasn't it?
s / We did a fake Foale and Tuffin card. 'Something and Nuffin', about eight of them, Tom [Stoppard] helped us do it.
m / Yes, there was a whole load of them, silly names.
s / With all the logo back to front, round the wrong way or things in the wrong places.

**So when you did your collection on your own Sally, it was almost the same label but without Marion's name.**

s / Yes, I just took Marion Foale off.

**Fundamentally Foale and Tuffin clothes were very simple in shape and silhouette but the detailing and the 'hardware', the buttons, buckles and lace were really important.**

m / It was really thought about, and we were always looking for new ideas like great D-rings

or 1930s buttons.
s / We found old ones that we had copied.
m / In those days there was Trim Fit and there was Klein and there was Schwenk, all based in London. And I think Schwenk are the only ones still there.
s / Some were definitely old stock, authentic 1930s buttons. Some we ordered and had made specially for us.
m / And there was a place in Berwick Street that did a lot of old lace, and Borowicks, which is still there.
s / Yes a lot of the lace was old stock.
m / And then the studs and cowboy stuff. We liked all that workwear and cowboy stuff; very functional.

**What about the photographers and editors and their interpretation of your designs? Obviously Marit [Allen] did a lot of things with you in the beginning – the 'About Twenty' pages with Caterine Milinaire and 'Young Ideas' – and also she wore your things. That photo shoot in Vogue: was that a relationship that was really important to you, having her on the inside so to speak?**

m / Oh yes, yes.
s / We were doing it before we met her and she just said, 'This is what I want!'
m / Like she found other people as well. She would search people out.
s / Yes, she would always find a shop that nobody went to and drag you there to see it.
m / She was a little bit younger but we were all looking at the same things, wanting the same things, excited by the same things.
s / At the same nightclubs, the same places to go and hang out.

**And then there were those iconic photographs of Twiggy. The Helmut Newton pictures with the cat, and then the Cecil Beaton ones.**

m / With the fringing.

**And then the Traeger shot.**

m / On the little bike with the spotty look.

**Was she right for your clothes?**

m / Well, she was the right look.
s / I remember we used to always fight over a certain look of model like Marie-Lise Gres and Jenny Boyd, who was our house model.
m / Twiggy was perfect for the time.

**At that time she had just broken through.**

m / Yes, it was early in her career.

**And then Marianne Faithfull, photographed by Bailey. In the credits it says she is wearing the 'Policeman's jacket'.**

m / Yes, it was called 'Fuzz'. We used to name things to suit.

**Like the 'Christopher Robin' jacket.**

m / That was Dormeuil tweed with velvet.

**And was naming things part of the fun, or did you think of it as marketing?**

m / No, we just didn't want to number things because numbers can get muddled up, and then it became quite fun. I still do it with every sweater. They have a name.

**It gives them a personality.**

s / Yes, you can see why that was called the 'Christopher Robin' jacket and why the policeman's jacket was called 'Fuzz'. I didn't realise they put the names in as well.

**And Julie Christie wearing letter dresses that spelt out her name.**

m / That was the sportswear time, and the running dress.
s / It was the Olympics, and we did T-shirt dresses.
m / But they asked us to make them specifically for the photo shoot.
s / We did one with a Y on it.
m / Our Y-fronts.
s / And didn't we know her?

Didn't we go round that tiny little flat?
m / Wasn't that Susannah York?
s / No, Julie Christie. Somebody I knew went out with her and we used to go round her flat, a third-floor flat in a block.

**And then Baby Jane Holzer, the American socialite and Warhol starlet, raved about your boutique and was quite taken with a Yorkshire terrier in the window. Whose dog was that?**

s / Ben, my dog. He was given to me by one boyfriend, and the second boyfriend, which was Richard, had to put up with a dog that he absolutely loathed. (both laugh)
m / And if you went away then I looked after him. I remember, when you first had him was when Marit and Caterine used to come around to the studio, and it was really cold and we used to have a little blow heater on the floor and he would curl up in front of it.

**Much later, in 1971, Pat Cleveland modelled your designs in 'Vogue'.**

s / That was when she wore the dungarees back to front. It had a bib. It was multicoloured satin. Was that Foale and Tuffin?
m / No, that was you. It's not F&T.
s / It might be?
m / I don't think it was
s / [reads credit in *Vogue*] 'Quilted red and yellow satin dungarees, red satin frill blouse, Foale and Tuffin!'
m / Oh, ok, must have been. At Countdown.
s / But that definitely wasn't the front .
m / I remember doing satin quilting, and we did velvet quilting. It was obviously a follow-through from the Japanese look, but shiny.

**Your things did go from the very simple little dresses to, in 1964, the sparkly Lurex 'discotheque dress'.**

S / We did lots like that, didn't we. We did them with stripes.
M / The 'discotheque dress'; what a lovely name.
S / Very much a 'discotheque dress'.

**You always said that you wanted your dresses to be about dancing. And it was always quite simple.**

S / It wasn't about being smart or going over the top.
M / No, we were always about dressing down.

**Even with a Lurex evening dress.**

M / Yes, it could be shiny or lace but you dressed down.
S / And it wasn't about conspicuous consumption.

**And about four years later it suddenly became more elegant and 1940s in style.**

S / I don't know why we did that.
M / Yes, we did do a forties suit with the stripe panels. That was the tree bark crêpe, and there was another rayon crêpe we bought from Cavendish textiles. We bought up a load of tree bark crêpe that was ex-stock that they were getting rid of.
S / Perhaps we were preparing ourselves for the softer 'Summer of Love'.

**Maybe you were just ahead of your time. The whole early seventies was about nostalgia and glam, Antony Price and Biba. The early sixties began as very optimistic, but by the end of it things had started to fall apart. You thought you could change the world, but things just didn't really happen like that. And the early 1970s was very grey.**

S / Yeah, we sort of grew up then. We had babies in the early seventies.
M / Yes.
S / I was married in 1969. It was probably something to do with having families and growing up.

M / I had Polly in 1972.
S / When did Marit get married? We did the whole or most of Marit's trousseau, and it was all very soft and feminine, silk jersey and softer shapes.
M / And the 'Muddy Waters' velvet trouser suit.

**The same Napoleonic jacket?**

M / Well, yes, but it was single-breasted. It would have been the same block as one called 'Kit'.
S / Because we actually found a Balenciaga block that was jolly useful. And when Baby Jane Holzer asked us to take her clothes to New York for her we realised that one of them was a Chanel jacket, which had this extraordinary sleeve, and we tried to figure out how it was cut and I think we took a pattern from it. Do you remember that?
M / Yeah, I do.
S / And it wasn't just a normal sleeve, it was curved.
M / It was moulded, and we were just learning how to do all that, really sculpted tailoring.

**It became much more sophisticated.**

S / Maybe we were just growing up.
M / And the timing was important. We had to do it because fashion was going that way.

**Two years later it got even more feminine. Gypsy dresses and embroidered smocks. Very pastoral and pretty.**

M / That was the silk voile.
S / I think this was the beginning of the hippy kaftan look. That was the one that Jo Bergman was stuck in, in the changing room. She couldn't get in or out of that dress.

**It was very romantic.**

S / I think we were influenced by early smocks and kaftans. I went to Egypt.
M / That was that embroidered smock that farmers used to wear.

**It has that 'Tess of the D'Urbervilles' feeling that obviously Laura Ashley made her own in the early 1970s. That whole Victoriana thing that people picked up at markets.**

S / But you didn't know why you did it. That's the odd thing. I didn't know why I went to Egypt, I didn't know why I fell in love with kaftans and brought them back. It wasn't ever planned.
M / I don't know why I fell in love with trouser suits.
S / Well, it was probably because we weren't allowed to wear trousers at art school, that's why.
M / But I do remember buying an actual pattern of a farmer's smock that you could embroider, with all the transfers and exactly how you make it, from that shop in Regent Street, Needlewoman. I've still got one of those and it's beautiful.
S / There was a knock-on thing, if you collected vintage or quilts or smocks or kaftans and they were embroidered.

**But throughout your career your look remained not overly dressed up.**

S / I think it had something to do with what part of your body you use. When you went to clubs the movement used to be all about shrugging your shoulders, that kind of dance that Twiggy did with her skinny little shoulders. And then later it was more flipping your hips. Why did we do hipster trousers? Because it was sort of strutting and cowboyish?
M / Cowboy. Yes, cowboy. I can remember going out to dinner and I couldn't think what to wear, and I ended up putting on black satin flared trousers and a black top. Really, really simple. And when I went out, Barbara Hulanicki was eating in the same restaurant and I felt very chic, yet I couldn't have been more dressed down.
S / It was so important because houses were like that, quite minimalist, it was the first scrubbed floor era.

**At the beginning there was that link with pop art, and a real crossover between art and fashion. You have even been described as, 'the Peter Blake of fashion'. Obviously you know him.**

s / How did we meet Peter? It must have been through Derek.

m / Probably through Derek Boshier because we knew Derek Boshier pretty well because he was the boyfriend of Pauline Fordham, who worked for us.

s / Derek was at art school with us?

m / No, I don't remember that, because the fashion school was separate to the fine art school, but we met in the dining hall and the bar.

s / But I remember Peter much earlier, and just going around his house and filling in bits of his paintings.

m / And just talking with them, hanging out and socialising with them because it was the Royal College of Art.

s / Yes, the common room. That was where we used to hang out and you would get a meal for 2s 6d and they had a very good bar too.

m / It was good fun and we only lived round the corner. We used to get totally drunk. I remember I was so drunk one day that I was standing at the bar talking to the barman, and I was eating crisps, and without realising it … you know you used to get a packet of crisps with a twist of blue paper with salt in it? Well, I ate that too!

s / And there was the Temperance Seven. Did they go to the RCA?

m / They always played at the Royal College. I think some of them went there but they always played there. That bar was good fun.

**And Peter Blake's first wife?**

m / Jann Haworth. She was an artist as well and made those dolls.

**Did she wear your clothes?**

s / We made her wedding dress.

m / The lace dress with the keyhole at the neckline.

s / With the round neck and little collar.

m / And then Natalie Gibson [textile designer] turned up at the wedding in the same dress and took it off and borrowed a big jumper from Peter. In fact Tom Stoppard's first wife, Josie wore that dress as well.

s / No, we made her a suit. It wasn't a dress.

**When you started, you were very young?**

m / We were completely naive.

s / We thought we knew everything, and we had no experience at all.

**There's a quote I love from an early newspaper article: 'We're young. We know!'** (both laugh)

m / We're young. We know! That was typical. We were horrible.

**But that arrogance of youth also allows you to do things. Barbara [Hulanicki] says that part of it was not knowing how to do things, you just did it.**

m / Yes. Worked your way through it.

s / Well actually, we did know how to do it.

m / We knew how to cut and make things. We knew all that.

s / We were very well trained, I think.

m / But we didn't know the business side of things.

s / No, not at all.

m / Hadn't got a clue.

s / And we didn't have husbands or accountants like they all did. It's not fair.

m / Perhaps that was a good thing.

**But you had each other.**

m / It did happen like that. If one was down the other was up and it would switch round. It must be very difficult to keep doing it on your own when you're having a bad day.

**But those early days were an incredibly optimistic time.**

m / Yes.

s / You know, there was Tom Stoppard writing for a boring newspaper.

m / He did *Mrs Dale's Diary* as well.

s / And you never thought you'd get anywhere and then suddenly it all happened and you were taken to the most amazing places. And the same thing with The Beatles, suddenly they were given MBEs.

m / Didn't they send them back, or was that just John Lennon?

**But by the end of the sixties and early seventies you were more grown-up and it had become a business. Did it take its toll?**

s / Not that I can remember. For some reason there were always orders.

m / It wasn't really a problem.

s / But it wasn't that Paraphernalia was always going to like what you were doing, or that the Browns orders would always be coming in. We were just amazingly lucky. We used to go to Paris and we'd buy shoes and have a lot of fun, be totally irresponsible, but we actually managed to make a boutique in Paris buy our clothes. In fact, I think there were two. And we used to go over there and take our clothes in a suitcase.

m / But that's youth, isn't it.

s / And a sense of humour.

m / Yes.

s / The worse things got, the more you laughed. And we had our health, wealth and happiness. (both laugh)

m / Well, I wouldn't say we had wealth.

s / We didn't have wealth, did we?

m / That was the last thing we had.

**What in the end made you decide to split up?**

m / I think you come to that point where, well, we'd grown up; we started to have fellas and babies. Sally stayed in London, but I went to the Midlands. I met a guy from the Midlands on the beach.

s / Marion was on holiday and met this man.

m / He was quite a lot younger than me.

**So then the label was dissolved. Did you shut up the shop?**

m / No, Sally carried on.

s / No, Marion just walked away.

m / I went. I went to live in the Midlands. I was just about to get married. And then Polly was born nine months to the day.

s / Your mother must have been pleased. (both laugh)

**Sally, you carried on. The first collection, I think, was the polka dots.**

m / The 'clowny' one.

s / Yes, because I was pregnant by then.

**I want to end by going right back to the beginning again. In 1962, at the very start, you were quoted in the 'Daily Mirror' as saying, 'A dress or a suit isn't fashion, a look is'. What look would you say best sums up Foale and Tuffin?**

m / Gosh, there's more than one look!

s / It would be leggy. It's slim; short haircuts; boyish?

m / Trendy.

s / I do think it was the beginning of the androgynous look, and you would never wear a twinset and pearls. Ever.

m / It was the essence of the sixties, and what that young person was.

s / I think it was a working girl who lived very simply, had short haircuts and no blow-dry, no rollers, no suspenders.

m / The Foale and Tuffin girl was active, working, trendy and probably lived in London.

s / But it wasn't important to show wealth.

**M** / No, absolutely. I think also we wanted things to be functional.

**You were about living the life.**

**M** / We were living the life. We wanted to move about, we didn't want to be trussed up with corsets.

**And even when it was glamorous, like the slip dress you did for Susannah York, it wasn't overly dressed up.**

**S** / But that was her choice. That's not what we [originally] made her.
**M** / We loved what we made her.
**S** / We made her something really simple in white jersey that hung straight.
**M** / Rayon jersey.
**S** / And it had white and gold sequins.
**M** / Silver and gold.
**S** / A geometric shoulder thing.
**M** / And down the side was split up.
**S** / It was a really cracking dress, but it wasn't sexy, so we had to make that satin dress.
**M** / That was the only one she didn't like that we did.
**S** / That's true.
**M** / So we had to end up doing something that she wanted. The bias cut slip. Clingy. Sexy.
**S** / And she made a very good case for it. She wanted to look like a film star.

**And it was very vampy.**

**M** / Yes, it was sexy. She knew what she wanted. But we were very disappointed.
**S** / We were.
**M** / We weren't used to being told what to do.
**S** / No.

(both laugh)

Sally (left) and Marion model
their Y-front dresses, 'photograph
defaced by staff', 1964.

**Overleaf:**
Hippy Marion (left), hippy
Sally (right), 1971, *Sunday Times/
Fashion Museum, Bath*.

211

## Marit Allen

A fashion editor who produced the innovative 'About 20' pages for *Queen* magazine before becoming 'Young Ideas' editor at *Vogue*. She played a vital role in championing young British designers during the 1960s and '70s. Allen became a costume designer for film, with credits including *Kaleidoscope* (1966), *Don't Look Now* (1973) and *Brokeback Mountain* (2005). She was married to Sandy Lieberson until 1983. Allen died in 2007.

## Sylvia Ayton

Student with Foale and Tuffin at Walthamstow School of Art and the Royal College of Art (RCA). During the 1960s Ayton set up The Fulham Road Clothes Shop in partnership with Zandra Rhodes. From 1969 she was outerwear designer at Wallis for thirty-three years. In 1990 she was awarded an MBE. She now acts as external examiner for various BA fashion courses, and is chairman of the Costume Society.

## Caroline Baker

Influential stylist and fashion editor of *Nova* magazine in the late 1960s and '70s. Masterminded iconic fashion images popularising fitness workout clothing and army surplus chic, featured in *Cosmopolitan*, *Tatler* and *The Face*. She is currently fashion editor at *You* magazine, *Mail on Sunday*.

## Jo Bergman

Personal assistant to Mick Jagger, Bergman ran the Rolling Stones offices in London and the South of France. She is now a writer living in Pasadena, California.

## Jane Best

Worked with Foale and Tuffin as a sample machinist in the 1960s. Today she continues to work alongside Marion in her present Hand Knitwear Design Company. She now lives in Warwickshire with her two cats.

## Manolo Blahnik

One of the world's most influential footwear designers. Blahnik graduated from the University of Geneva in 1965 and studied art in Paris. Encouraged by Diana Vreeland, he launched his career in 1971 designing shoes for Ossie Clark. His name has become an international brand. He was awarded an honorary CBE in 2007. He lives in London near his flagship store in Chelsea.

## Peter Blake

The pioneering 'godfather' of British pop art attended the Royal College of Art 1953-56. Best known for his iconic cover of The Beatles' 1967 album, *Sergeant Pepper's Lonely Hearts Club Band*. In 1975 he moved to Somerset and was a founding member of the Brotherhood of Ruralists. He received a knighthood in 2002. He now lives in West London where he continues to produce works inspired by popular culture.

## Sandy Boler

Joined *Vogue* in 1962 as a young fashion editor in charge of gloves, corsets, lingerie and wedding dresses, and started the 'More Dash Than Cash' pages. She is now retired, writing freelance on travel and other subjects. She lives in Brixton and Somerset with her husband Adrian.

## Derek Boshier

Studied at the RCA. A key member of the British pop art movement alongside David Hockney, Allen Jones and Peter Blake. His graphic artwork has been commissioned by musicians David Bowie and The Clash. He is a respected lecturer and continues to produce acclaimed shows. He lives and works in Los Angeles.

## Jenny Boyd

Foale and Tuffin's house model. She was part of the 'Youthquake' fashion shows in New York. She is now an author working in the addiction field and organising workshops for people on a journey of self-discovery. She lives with her husband in England and spends part of the year in Los Angeles with her children and grandchildren.

## Joan Burstein

Opened Browns fashion boutique in London with her husband Sidney in 1970, and is known for her talent spotting. Foale and Tuffin were among the first British designers Mrs B (as she is fondly known) bought: the Chinese and Clown Liberty print collections. Awarded a CBE in 2006, Mrs B is still at Browns and is about to celebrate forty years since the doors first opened.

## Caroline Charles

Fashion designer Charles dressed pop icons Lulu and Marianne Faithfull, and was herself a guest on *Juke Box Jury*. She established her own label in October 1963. Currently her company has eleven retail shops, wholesales in the UK, and exports. She was awarded an OBE in 2002.

## Grace Coddington

Won British *Vogue* Young Model Competition at eighteen. Joined the magazine as a fashion editor in 1968. She is now creative director of American *Vogue* and lives with hairdresser Didier Malige and a menagerie of cats.

## Terence Conran

One of the world's best-known designers, restaurateurs and retailers. He founded Habitat in 1964 and is today the chairman of the Conran Group, which has shops, restaurants and hotels around the world and an international architecture and design practice.

## Vanessa Denza

Original buyer for the Woollands 21 shop where Foale and Tuffin started their career. She owns Denza, an international fashion consultancy and recruitment business, co-founded Graduate Fashion Week and was awarded an MBE in 2004 for her services to the British fashion industry and fashion education.

## Lesley Ebbetts

Fashion editor of the *Daily Mirror* and *Rave* magazine. During her career, stylist and writer Ebbetts has contributed to numerous periodicals. She was TV's first 'live' fashion expert, featured on Richard and Judy's *This Morning* show. She currently works as a freelance fashion editor and consultant and lives in Buckinghamshire.

## Sally Fleetwood

Creator of the label Sally Jess Ltd, she designed unique handbags using futuristic new materials (including Perspex and PVC) to go with the collections of London's top young fashion designers. These became iconic of the period. Jesse also ran the Foale and Tuffin shop. She now lives in the chapel she converted in Cornwall with her partner, the painter David Andrew.

## Felicity Green

In the 'Swinging Sixties', award-winning journalist Green was responsible for the witty fashion pages in the *Daily Mirror* (now part of the V&A Museum's permanent archive). She became the first woman to be appointed to the board of a national newspaper group when the *Daily Mirror* was selling over five million copies a day. She has contributed to numerous magazines and inspired a new generation, teaching fashion journalism at Central St Martins.

# Cast of characters

### Celia Hammond
A model throughout the sixties, she has been running the Celia Hammond Animal Trust (CHAT), based in Wadhurst, East Sussex, for over twenty years. CHAT runs low-cost neuter clinics and treatment centres in London, a twenty-four-hour emergency service for sick and injured strays, a rescue and rehoming service, and sanctuary accommodation in the country.

### Barbara Hulanicki
Originally worked as a fashion illustrator for publications including the *Sunday Times*, *Women's Wear Daily* and *Vogue*. In 1964, with her late husband Stephen Fitz-Simon, she founded the influential fashion label Biba. Her mail-order fashion business grew into a fashion empire housed in a five-storey department store in Kensington High Street. She now lives in Miami, where she works as an interior designer.

### John Jesse
In 1965 he opened the first gallery to specialise in art nouveau and art deco. In the same year he launched an innovative range of flower and op art print shirts. These sold in Paraphernalia, Woollands and Austin Reed. In 1966 he introduced Sally Tuffin to her future husband Richard Dennis. He now deals in art nouveau and art deco by appointment.

### Betsey Johnson
Fashion editor and illustrator at *Mademoiselle* magazine, Johnson became one of the most imaginative and publicised young designers for the Paraphernalia store. The creator of 'Canned Panties', Jackie Kennedy and Julie Christie wore her designs. In 1978 she launched her own label, which she continues to showcase at New York Fashion Week today.

### Brigid Keenan
Born in India and educated in convents in Britain, Keenan's career has ranged from being assistant editor at *Nova*, women's editor at the *Observer* and 'Young Fashion' editor at the *Sunday Times*. She is now an author of titles including *The Women We Wanted to Look Like*, *Dior in Vogue* and *Diplomatic Baggage: The Adventures of a Trailing Spouse*.

### Sandy Lieberson
Hollywood agent, film producer, movie studio executive, devoted friend and dedicated admirer of Foale and Tuffin.

### Gerald McCann
Studied at the RCA under Madge Garland. He began his fashion career with Marks & Spencer. His own label designs sold to Bazaar, Woollands 21 Shop, Bergdorf Goodman, Bloomingdale's and Peter Robinson. One of the original 'Swinging London' trendsetters photographed for *Life* magazine by Norman Parkinson, McCann is a renowned raconteur. He is now retired and 'behaving himself'.

### Meriel McCooey
Held the position of fashion editor at the *Daily Express*, the *Observer* and the *Sunday Times* magazine. She is now retired and spends her time between homes in London and France.

### Caterine Milinaire
Along with Marit Allen, fashion editor Milinaire co-edited the 'About 20' youth-orientated fashion pages in *Queen* magazine, c.1963-64. Milinaire is now a photojournalist for magazines and books. She lives and works in Newport, Rhode Island, America.

### Bernard Nevill
Studied and taught at St Martins School of Art and the Royal College of Art, where he became professor of textiles. His collaborations with Liberty as a fabric designer and colour consultant revitalised the brand. Nevill's legendary 'trend antennae' inspired many fashions of the day, specifically his groundbreaking Islamic and art deco prints. A one-time *Vogue* contributor, he now works as a design consultant and continues to lecture.

### Molly Parkin
Pioneering fashion editor of *Nova*, *Harpers & Queen* and the *Sunday Times*. In 1949 Parkin won scholarships to Brighton and Goldsmiths College of Art. She began her career in fashion making hats and bags for Barbara Hulanicki. The flamboyant iconoclast has contributed to numerous publications, written novels and appeared in a one-woman show. She has now returned to her first love: painting.

### Mary Quant
Influential fashion designer who changed fashion and beauty forever in the sixties with her miniskirts, hipsters and hot pants. She revolutionised make-up with her first collection in 1965, with unheard of colours and techniques still used today. She studied at Goldsmiths College where she met her husband Alexander Plunkett-Green and together they launched Bazaar in the Kings Road, which provided a template for a new retail culture. She was awarded an OBE in 1966. In 2000 she sold her companies to the Japanese and she remains a consultant to them in an advisory capacity.

### Monica Renaudo
Production manager for Foale and Tuffin Ltd, now living in Dorset and the South of France with husband André.

### Zandra Rhodes
Foale and Tuffin were the first dress designers to use Rhodes' textile prints when she left the RCA in 1964. Her design empire now includes couture dresses, shoes, greetings cards and a collection for Marks and Spencer, and she designs sets and costumes for the opera. She was awarded a CBE in 1997 and later founded the Fashion and Textile Museum (FTM) in London. She now lives between London and San Diego, California with her partner Salah Hassanein.

### May Routh
Fashion illustrator, designer, model and manageress of the Foale and Tuffin boutique, Routh left England in 1974, and headed for America with Brian Eatwell. She started a new life and career as a costume designer in film and TV, including *The Man Who Fell to Earth* (1974) and *Splash* (1984). She now lives in Los Angeles.

### Jean Shrimpton
One of the iconic faces of the sixties. The model, nicknamed 'The Shrimp', appeared on the covers of numerous magazines, from *Woman's Weekly* and *Glamour* to *Vogue* and *Harper's Bazaar*. A central character in the swinging London 'In Crowd', she famously dated photographer David Bailey and actor Terence Stamp. She now runs a hotel in Cornwall.

### Pauline Smith (née Denyer)
At Foale and Tuffin, Denyer worked as a sample maker and pattern grader. She then became the other half of Paul Smith Ltd. Now Paul Smith's other half, she lives in London.

### Janet Street Porter
Studied architecture at the Architectural Association before becoming a Fleet Street columnist and fashion writer at twenty-one. Since 1973 she has worked in radio and television and her maverick style won her a BAFTA in 1988. Author, presenter, newspaper editor, renowned rambler and 'Grumpy Old Woman', she is one of Britain's best-known media celebrities.

### James Wedge
Long-time friend and collaborator of Foale and Tuffin. During his career Wedge progressed from being London's top milliner to Kings Road boutique owner (Countdown and Top Gear) to fashion photographer working for *Nova*, *Vogue*, *19* and the *Sunday Times* magazine. He is now a figurative painter living in Dorset.

**In 1972, I settled into family life** in a sixteenth-century thatched farmhouse on the Warwickshire borders living the 'good life', growing vegetables, keeping goats and enjoying a little knitting in the evenings – just making it up as I went along. By 1978 and two children later, I realised we needed extra income and had noted a desire for hand knitwear in the world of fashion.

Working from home, I set about teaching myself to write a properly functioning and accurate pattern, which took me about a year to complete in longhand! When I had finally conquered this, I designed a capsule collection of jumpers and cardigans, which a close friend photographed for me.

Where to go from there? Marit Allen suggested I sell hand knitwear as a wholesale range. I showed it to Paul Smith, who was a good friend of mine. Paul said no, he felt it would not work, as it was too classic and understated. People wanted sweaters with patterns of flowers or sheep on them! We laugh about that hiccup to this day.

Undaunted, I took this small range and showed it to Meriel McCooey, who was the fashion editor of the *Sunday Times* colour supplement, and whom I had known from my Foale and Tuffin days. Meriel selected one piece for the magazine, offering it as a free pattern. They were inundated with requests, so I knew then there was a market for my look.

The timing was excellent, as it became apparent that not only was hand knitwear much in demand, but Vanessa Denza had started her business as a design agent for top retailers looking for something different. Almost immediately I found I was selling to stores in the America and England such as Whistles and Margaret Howell.

By now, my styling had progressed from conventional, two-dimensional designs to my own, totally new and different concept: sculptured three-dimensional designs, with special attention being paid to fine detail, stitch and finishing – inspired of course, by my love for tailoring, good cutting and shape.

In 1985, I produced a book called *Marion Foale's Classic Knitwear*, which became a much-loved bible for home knitting enthusiasts, and to this day, although out of print, is still going strong on eBay and in libraries.

Now, twenty-eight years on, we are working from premises in a historic town in the Midlands. We produce two collections a year and present them at London, New York and Paris Fashion Weeks, selling to top boutiques and stores around the world.

All this has been made possible by approximately three hundred talented local hand knitters and eight permanent staff, the majority having been with me for twenty years and more. We have now progressed not only to buying fine yarns of pure cotton and wool from around the world, but also to producing our very own special three-ply wool yarn, dyed in many colours of our choosing, which gives our garments a unique and special dimension.

*Thanks to Penny Badger for editing my copy.*

# Marion Foale

**I am impressed by Iain's energy** in sourcing so much detail of our lives in the sixties. Did we really make an impression on the fashion scene? If so, it wasn't intentional – a romp in the world of clothes, fuelled by stubbornness and dreams. I'm flattered to read that we have encouraged contemporary designers to take the plunge and go it alone – fashion is now all the stronger because of freethinking young designers.

When Marion left London in 1972, the label became Sally Tuffin Ltd. For another three years the firm continued in Ganton Street in much the same way as before, although it was lonely without Marion. I was still living in Notting Hill and newly married to Richard Dennis, a Kensington antique dealer. Wanting a greener, calmer lifestyle for ourselves and two young sons, we were lured to Somerset. Monica Renaudo, our Foale and Tuffin production manager, lived nearby, and in 1975 we started Tuppence Coloured, a mail-order firm selling ready-to-sew smocked and quilted children's clothes in Liberty prints. With babies on our knees, we spent hours in our kitchens compiling instruction sheets and knitting patterns.

Branching out into adult sizes, we dressed a rather shy and young Delia Smith for her very first television cookery programme. In 1978 we worked on a BBC series, *Children's Wardrobe*, presented by Ann Ladbury.

In 1981 my family survived a serious car crash – a life-changing event which caused us to re-evaluate our priorities and lifestyle. For the next five years I enjoyed a slower, more tranquil existence. Richard became involved with the famous but ailing Moorcroft Pottery; we bought a one-third share of the business. This led me to substitute cloth for clay – I was catapulted into designing pots as art director. We commuted from Somerset to Stoke-on-Trent. This was an echo of my early days in fashion. Thrown in to the deep end, my stubborn streak prevailed, battling to source new colours and shapes. With the support of John and Walter Moorcroft, I reworked the Pottery's celebrated house style, utilising the principles of pattern-cutting learned from fashion school. Once again, Moorcroft became a healthy, thriving company.

In 1992 we left Stoke-on-Trent. Poole Pottery was our next port of call; David Queensberry invited us to take part in the revival of traditional painting. Quite a learning curve and challenge – but the sea was on the doorstep. Again, as at Moorcroft, the camaraderie and generosity of the decorators carried us along. A highlight was a British Airways commission to adapt my design 'Dolphins and Seagulls' for the tail fins of aircraft in their fleet.

Since 1993 I have been designing pots for Dennis Chinaworks, our studio pottery in Somerset. We train local art students – it is very rewarding to watch the steps from faltering trainee to brilliant decorator. The transformation of a lump of grey clay into a glowing, colourful pot is so rewarding; I am completely hooked. Our pots attract an enthusiastic collectors' market, the success of which is reflected in a specially commissioned annual sale by Bonhams auction house in Bond Street, London – 2009 is our tenth year.

My great friend, Marit Allen, taught me to see fashion as an integral part of life: 'Search for new ideas. Keep looking fresh and cutting edge. See fashion as an investment.'

Our motto: 'Divide the price of the garment by the number of times you wear it.'

*Thanks to my sister Sue for proof-reading.*

# Sally Tuffin

Alice and Mary Temperley
modelling Tuppence
Coloured, 1980,
*Photo: Marit Allen.*

Poole Pottery designs
and the BA tail fin, 1997,
*Photo: Richard Dennis.*

Sally and Dennis
Chinaworks Leopard pot,
*Photo: Magnus Dennis.*

Moorcroft Carp vase,
70cms, 1991.

An Oral History of British Fashion
Quotation on pages 64-5 from Marit
Allen's interview in *An Oral History
of British Fashion* collection, catalogue
number C1046/13 © British Library
(www.bl.uk/oralhistory). Reproduced
with permission.

*Angela Carter Archive*
(exhibition catalogue)

Bracewell, Michael,
*Re-make, Re-model – Art, Pop,
Fashion and the making of Roxy Music
1953-1972* (Faber and Faber)

Carter, Ernestine,
*The Changing World of Fashion*
(Weidenfeld and Nicolson)

Connikie, Yvonne,
*Fashions of a Decade*
(B.T.Batsford Ltd)

Demilly, Christian,
*Pop Art: Adventures in Art* (Prestel)

Fogg, Marnie, Boutique –
*A '60s Cultural Phenomenon*
(Mitchell Beazley)

Gardiner, Juliet,
*From the Bomb to the Beatles*
(Collins & Brown)

Grunenberg, Christoph, & Laurence
Sillars, *Peter Blake, A Retrospective*
(Tate Publishing)

Harris, Jennifer, Sarah Hyde
& Greg Smith, *1966 And All That*
(Trefoil Books Ltd)

Hulanicki, Barbara, *From A to Biba*
(V&A Publishing)

Jackson, Lesley,
*The Sixties: Decade of Design
Revolution* (Phaidon)

Larocca, Amy, *House of Mod*
(nymag.com)

Lester, Richard,
*John Bates: Fashion Designer*
(ACC Editions)

Levy, Shawn, *Ready, Steady, Go!:
Swinging London and the Invention
of Cool* (Fourth Estate)

Mansell, Colette, *The History of Sindy*
(New Cavendish Books)

Perry, George, *London in the Sixties*
(Pavillion)

Quant, Mary, *Quant by Quant*
(Pan Books)

Smith, Adam, *Now You See Her –
Pauline Boty, First Lady of British Pop*
(www.writing-room.com)

Twiggy, *Twiggy – An autobiography*
(Hart-Davis, MacGibbon)

Vermorel, Fred & Judy, *Sex Pistols:
The Inside Story* (Omnibus Press)

**FOALE & TUFFIN LTD**
4 Ganton Street London W1
tel. 01-437 3832   01-437 4581
Shop: 1 Marlborough Court
London W1   tel. 01-437 0087

# Bibliography

Just as it should be with any worthwhile project, the making of this book has been at times exhilarating and maddening, illuminating and frustrating. Throughout this process it has been my aim that the end result now in your hands might encourage a new generation of stylish upstarts (entrepreneurs and amateurs alike) to emulate the sixties spirit encapsulated by the crazy Foale and Tuffin girls and their creative cohort, and be inspired to explore a new world of possibilities.

I cannot begin to thank enough the remarkable contributors who were such a key part of the Foale and Tuffin family; from the tight-knit team that worked with them daily in their studio and boutique to the colleagues and associates who played a role in constructing or cataloguing their world. I am so thrilled that they managed to take the time to share their recollections. It has been a real treat to converse with such stylish, iconic individuals who between them fashioned an era. This book is very much their story too.

I must acknowledge the tireless efforts of the legions of personal assistants who organised the often tricky logistics of such a project as this.

While researching this book I have enjoyed many days in the excellent libraries at Central Saint Martins College of Art and Design and the London College of Fashion, along with the British Library (I recommend every fashion student to join now and take the opportunity to explore the newspaper archive at Colindale). I would also like to thank Susannah Hecht and all the editorial and production staff at ACC Publishing Group; Emily Snow, Caroline Ness and Elaine Uttley at the Fashion Museum, Bath; the *Vogue* Picture Library; IPC Magazines; National Magazine Syndication; and Delilah Khomo, for additional research produced with stylish aplomb.

During the making of this book it has been a delight to meet Richard Dennis, Sally's husband, and I have valued his cheerful optimism and steely vision. I thank him for the endless cups of tea and the odd lift to Yeovil train station. I would also like to thank Sally's sons, Magnus and Buchan, for helping produce several of the stunning images featured within the pages.

I have a huge debt of gratitude to the photographers who have generously given us permission to reproduce their wonderfully vital images, and I would very much like to thank Simon Cryer at Northbank Design for creating such an exciting, beautiful-looking book that matches my every expectation (no mean feat).

This book would not have been possible without two people. Rosemary Harden from the Fashion Museum in Bath has become a dear friend and an inspiring colleague. Her knowledge, keen research and enthusiasm have helped keep this book on the road. I also thank her for access to the museum's periodical collection and for the reproduction of several images from Ernestine Carter's *Sunday Times* archive.

I am also indebted to Matthew Freedman, who has managed my maverick authorship style with great generosity of spirit and good humour. He is the perfect collaborator who has made the creation of this book a joy, even in the dark moments. He will be forever John Steed to my Tara King.

And finally I would like to say a big thank you to Marion and Sally who are in every way the original inspiration for the book. I am happy that the two bolshy women who lived the fashion dream are still just that.

*For my brothers – John, Paul, David and Rex.*

# Acknowledgements

223